Submarines

Submarines

Richard Garrett

Little, Brown and Company
Boston   Toronto

Library of Congress
Catalog Card No. 77–89103

First American Edition

Printed in England

Contents

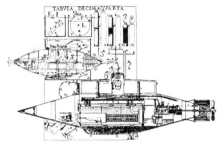

The Navies of the world have decreed that, although submarines are called boats, nuclear submarines are ships.
LEN DEIGHTON, *Spy Story*

In two World Wars, and in the military effort needed to prevent a third, a few hundred submarines, manned by a few thousand officers and men, at a cost of less than one per cent of the total expenditure on armaments, including research and development, have been a strategic factor of potentially decisive importance.
REAR ADMIRAL I. L. M. MCGEOCH, CB, DSO, DSC, RN

Introduction

It was, I think Disraeli who said that one should never explain or excuse. Since a certain amount of explanation is necessary to most books (why, otherwise, have introductions?), there is no need to deal with that part of his advice. However, I am very much aware that it is a poor thing to begin with excuses. My only reason is that they are an essential courtesy to anyone and anything not mentioned in these pages.

It would require a very long book to do complete justice to submarines. The subject has, after all, at least three facets. On the one hand, there is the far from simple truth that, in less than a century, they have developed from the crude ideas of eccentric inventors to large vessels travelling at high speed beneath the waves – and able to exist almost indefinitely without a sight of the sky.

This is the story of a technical masterpiece and how it grew. But there is also the effect of the submarine on history; of how, in two wars, it came near to starving Britain to death – and of how, nowadays, it has become the ultimate deterrent against a nuclear attack. This, on its own, is material for a book; but there is also the third facet, the tale of men who have served in these vessels; of their courage and of the adventures that befell them. Here, indeed, is meat for one of the most exciting stories anyone could write.

In *Submarines*, I have tried to include a little of all three elements. I have, however, made no more than a passing reference to the gallant submariners of the Second World War who went about their business in small craft such as the British X-boats – doing damage to the opposition out of all proportion to their size. Nor have I dealt with peaceable submarines, which have literally plumbed the depths of the ocean – and which, nowadays, are playing such an important role in the quest for offshore oil.

But these are generalities. I should like to have told more stories about individual heroism – such as the occasion when HMS *Thrasher* surfaced after a heavy aerial bombardment. Two unexploded bombs were found lodged in her casing. The two men who removed them were afterwards awarded the Victoria Cross.

There was also the occasion when the submarine *Trident* dived for cover in a Norwegian fjord – and went on sinking by the stern. To get her back on to an even keel, her crew had to pass buckets of water from the after bilges to the forward compartments. She was now much deeper than her specifications allowed – while, at the same time, an intense aerial bombardment was going on. Somehow, after several agonizing hours, she was righted and eventually came safely to the surface.

Winston Churchill once said, 'Of all the branches of men in the Forces there is none which shows more devotion and faces grimmer perils than the submariners.' All the powers involved in the Second World War would have said much the same thing about their own men.

At the end of this book, there appears a list of some of the works I have consulted. I should like, however, to thank especially the librarians of the London Library and the Royal United Services Institute for Defence Studies, Commander James E. Wentz, USN – US Navy Public Affairs Officer in London, Commander Richard Sharpe, RN, for allowing me to visit HMS *Courageous*, and to Captain Robin Heath, RN who, several years ago, allowed me to spend a day at sea with him in HMS *Seascout* – and thus introduced me to the silent world beneath the waves.

RICHARD GARRETT
Tunbridge Wells

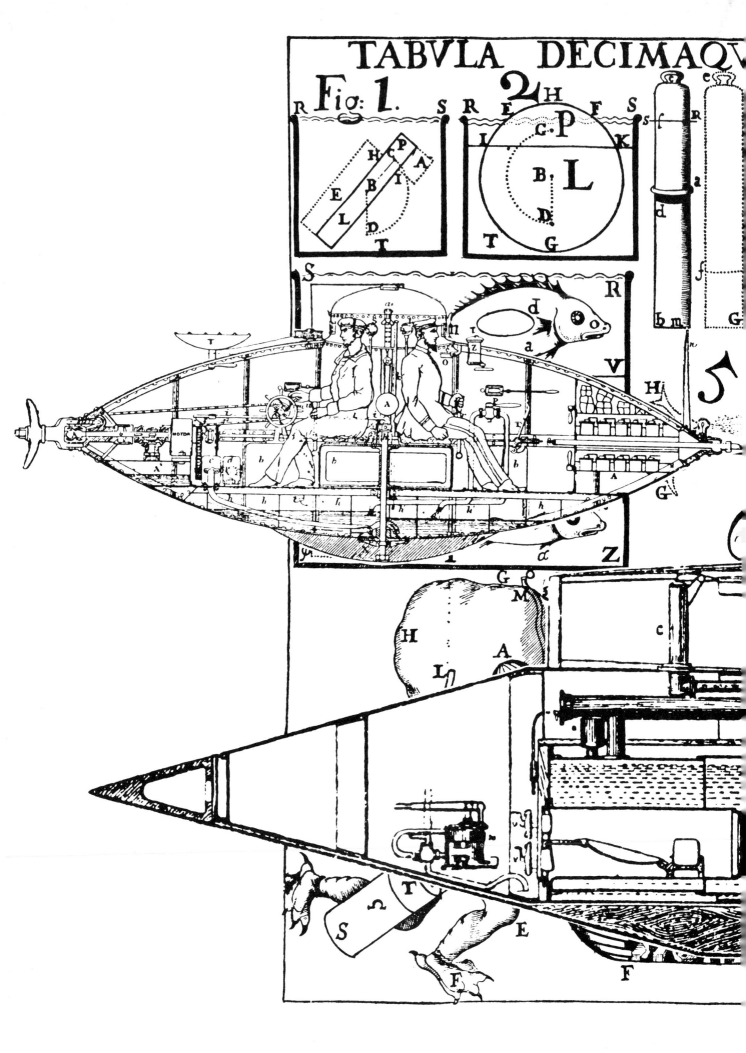

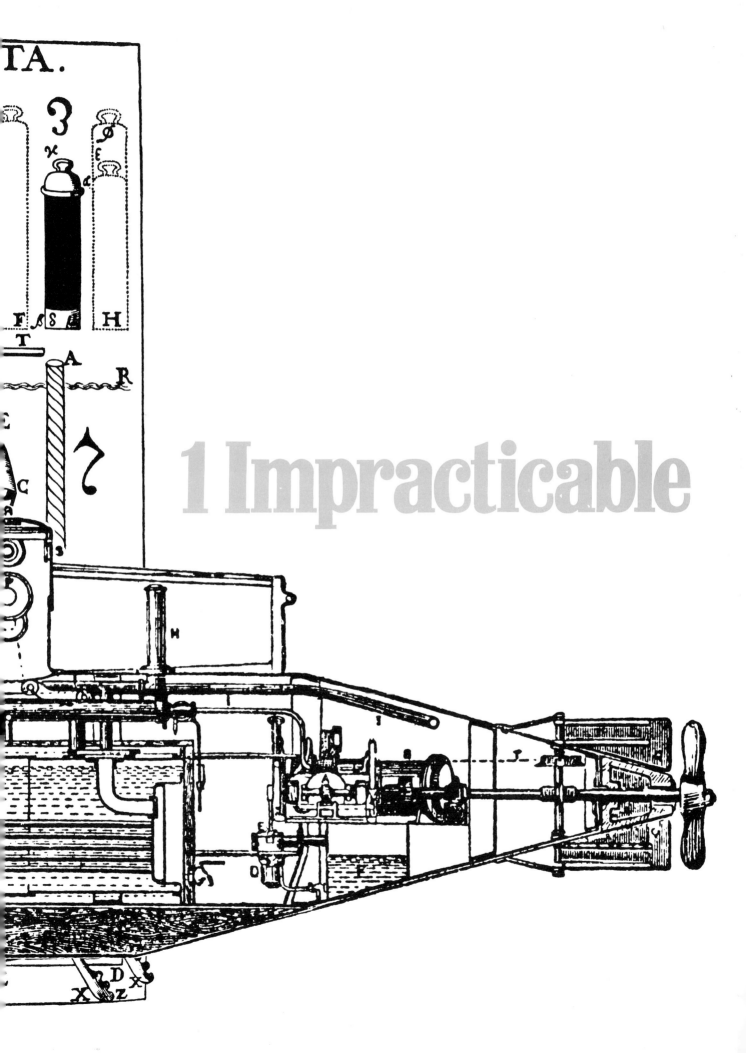

1 Impracticable

One of the factors separating the mind of *homo sapiens* from that of an animal is an awareness of limitations. Animals have a healthy regard for what is and isn't possible. They are practical creatures; they know where they belong and, by all appearances, they are content to remain there.

Mankind, on the other hand, has always entertained the wild idea that he should be free to move wherever he chooses. From the moment (or almost) he was placed upon earth, he assumed an entitlement to climb into the sky, and to explore the ocean. The fact that this right was obviously not a divine one was of small importance. What God had overlooked, man would have to accomplish on his own.

One of the first inventors to tackle the fish syndrome, which seems a reasonable way of putting it, was Leonardo da Vinci. Having produced designs for an aeroplane and a parachute, it was, perhaps, natural that he should direct his ingenuity from one element to another. The device, which occupied many pages of a notebook, was intended for underwater exploration, and took the form of a diving bell. Unfortunately, it was never put to the test.

Some years after da Vinci's visionary designs, an Englishman named William Bourne took up the challenge of the deep. Mr Bourne lived at Gravesend near London on the River Thames. By profession he was a carpenter and gunmaker; by inclination, a mathematician. During his life he published a number of almanacks, works on navigation, and, in 1578, *Inventions or Devices*. Among the contents was a chapter on how to build submarines.

Since William Bourne's life is thinly documented, there is no knowing whether he ever constructed such a device. But the words have a confident ring to them, and it seems quite likely that, had such a vessel been produced, it would have worked. The key to his creation was a double hull. The outer, manufactured from wood, had holes in the side to admit water. The inner, fabricated from leather, was manipulated by screw presses. Contracted, they created a gap between the two; water poured in through the ports, and the boat sank. To regain the surface, you simply unscrewed the presses. The leather hull was pushed against the wooden; the water was expelled and the vessel, thus lightened, rose to the top. That, at any rate, was the theory.

No doubt Mr Bourne's writings were read by a Dutch physician named Cornelius van Drebbel. Whilst the Dutchman seems to have been unimpressed by the idea of a double hull, he was quick to see the sense of using leather. Early

PREVIOUS PAGES Early submarines were a potpourri of ingenuity and imagination run rampant.

RIGHT It seems unlikely that the sixteenth-century carpenter William Bourne ever actually built his dream boat. But he had the right ideas. Within the wooden outer hull there was another made from leather. Retracted, it allowed water to enter the space in between, and the vessel sank. With the aid of presses, the water could be expelled and the boat would surface. That, at any rate was the theory.

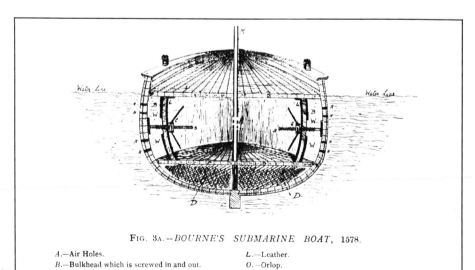

FIG. 3A.—*BOURNE'S SUBMARINE BOAT*, 1578.

A.—Air Holes.	L.—Leather.
B.—Bulkhead which is screwed in and out.	O.—Orlop.
C.—Capstan for screwing Bulkhead in and out.	M.—Hollow Mast for Air Supply.
D.—Ballast.	W.—Space occupied by Water when Craft is submerged
H.—Inlet Holes for Water.	S.—Screws.

in the next century he moved to London – where, beside the Thames, he worked on submersible boats. In 1620, he demonstrated one of them before an audience that included James I. According to some acounts, the monarch made a trip in it, but this seems unlikely. Whatever James's virtues were, the qualities required by a pioneer submariner were not among them.

The essence of van Drebbel's craft was a wooden hull, strengthened by iron bands and waterproofed by an outer leather skin. Manned by a crew of 12, it was equipped with 6 oars on either side. Apart from providing propulsion, they were supposed to act in the manner of a fish's fins – in other words, they kept the boat stable when submerged. Two sets of bellows, connected with the surface by tubes, ensured a circulation of reasonably fresh air. But the most important item in this respect was a substance discovered by van Drebbel. He called it 'quintessence of air'.

According to that eminent chemist, the Hon. Robert Boyle, 'when, from time to time, he perceived that the finer and purer part of the air was consumed, or even clogged by the respiration and steams of those that went in his ship, he would, by unstopping a vessel full of this liquor, speedily restore to the troubled air such a proportion of vital parts as would make it again for a good while fit for respiration'. Van Drebbel, whose secrecy was only marginally short of paranoiac, left no details of his magical prescription. Nor were the reporters of the day of very much help. Apart from giving substance to the idea of a submerged royal progress from Westminster to Greenwich, at least one claimed that the van Drebbel submersible had descended to a depth of 15 feet. This, clearly, was rubbish – at its deepest, it travelled only just beneath the surface.

Nevertheless, some people were impressed. The king was sufficiently enthusiastic to order 'boates to go under the water', though there is no evidence that they were ever built. What was more, when van Drebbel died in 1634, the significance of his work suddenly lit up. Almost immediately, an order was issued that 'none but kings successively and their heirs must know of it'. Ben Jonson, the contemporary poet laureate, enthused about

. . . an automa, runs under water
With a smug nose, and has a nimble tail
Made like an auger, with which tail she wriggles
Betwixt the costs of a ship and sinks it straight

Even allowing for a poet's imagination, it was an immense exaggeration. But Jonson was not the only writer who succumbed to van Drebbel's spell. John Wilkins, Bishop of Chester, in *Mathematical Magick* (1648), stepped into science fiction. Referring to a submarine as the 'Ark', he enthused about its immunity from attacks by pirates. Travelling at between five and six feet beneath the surface, it would be secure from the ravages of storms, ice, and tides. In war, enemy ships could be 'undermined in the water and blown up'. Strongholds close to the sea could be captured, and besieged garrisons supplied unseen. The opportunities for research and exploration were endless. Indeed, the bishop envisaged colonies of people living in these vessels – their 'children borne and bred up without the knowledge of land'. They would, presumably, live off fish; as for water, it could be obtained 'from the pure springs at the bottom of the ocean'.

If Bishop Wilkins's dreams trespassed into the fantastic, those of a Frenchman named de Son established some sort of a record for optimism. Long before his vessel was put to the test, he had published a catalogue of its accomplishments. 'The inventor of it doth undertake in one day', he wrote, 'to destroy 100 ships, can go from Rotterdam to London and back in one day, and in six

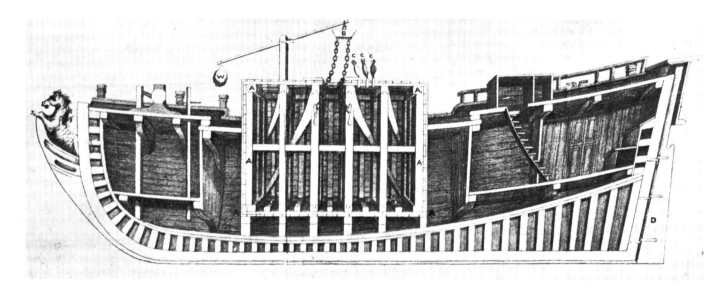

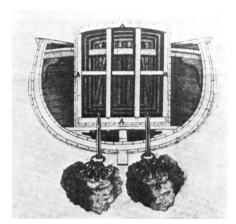

ABOVE AND BELOW Day's 1773 submarine. The idea of building a submersible sloop was ingenious. But at a depth of 150 fathoms the pressure was too much for the vessel and her luckless crew. There were no survivors.

weeks to go to the East Indies . . . Nor fire, nor storm, or bullets, can hinder, unless it please God.'

On paper, the de Son submarine was fit to make the world marvel. Its hull was 73 feet long; 12 feet high at the tallest point and 8 feet across at the widest. At either end, it tapered to a sharp point reinforced by a deadly iron ram. Its two cabins contained sufficient air to support life comfortably for three hours (not enough, surely, to go to the East Indies), but the real marvel was its means of locomotion. There was no nonsense about having to row it underwater; it was propelled by a giant paddle wheel powered by a clockwork motor. Fully wound, de Son explained, it would keep the vessel going for at least eight hours. What was more, it would provide a very acceptable turn of speed under water. With those vicious iron spikes, it could ram and sink the biggest English ship afloat.

De Son was the prototype public relations man. Such descriptions and promises titillated public imagination. When, one day in 1653, the submarine was due to be launched at Rotterdam, the notables of Holland turned up in strength. Alas – they were to be disappointed. Apologetically, de Son explained that certain materials had not arrived on time. The submarine was not *quite* ready. The occasion would have to be postponed.

Eventually, everything was in order and the boat was put into the water. The spectators held their collective breath – and so, apparently, did the submarine. Despite the fact that its clockwork motor was fully wound up, it did not move. In his enthusiasm, de Son had overlooked one vital fact. Whilst it rotated the paddle wheel perfectly well on dry land, it was less than a match for the pressure of water. It was a weakness for which there seemed to be no cure. De Son, far from going back to the drawing-board, turned his attention to some other device. The inert submarine became degraded to an amusing sideshow at country fairs.

Inattention to the pressure of water was also the undoing of an English carpenter named Day – though, in this case, the result was tragic. In 1773, Mr Day converted a small fishing boat into a crude submarine; sank it to a depth of 30 feet in the Norfolk Broads near Yarmouth, and presently returned triumphantly to the surface. This, he explained, was merely a modest beginning. If somebody would put up the money, he would show what he could really do. Alas – somebody did; £340 to be precise. With the cash in his pocket, Mr Day built what appeared to be a perfectly conventional sloop. The idea was that it should be submerged by means of two bundles of stones, held together by iron bands and suspended underneath.

When the boat was completed, he took it round the coast to Plymouth Sound, where he gave the first demonstration. True to his promise, the sloop sank; and, when the ballast was removed, it surfaced. The test had been carried out in comparatively shallow water. On 20 June 1774, he took the vessel to a point 300 yards from the shore. The water here, he said, was 150 fathoms deep. This would show the true wonder of his achievement.

At first, the boat seemed reluctant to co-operate. It remained stubbornly on the surface. Once extra ballast had been added, however, it appeared to give a small sigh. Then, gently, it went under.

The idea had been that Day would release some coloured floats when he reached the seabed. The crowd waited, but nothing appeared. People became anxious. Time spun out without the reappearance of Mr Day and his sloop. Presently HM frigate *Orpheus* was ordered to attempt a salvage operation. Her grapples made no contact with the doomed vessel; when the weather worsened, the search was called off.

Mr Day and his ill-fated vessel are still on the bed of Plymouth Sound. There is no knowing what exactly occurred, but there is no doubt about the disaster's cause. In the deeper water, the pressure became too much for the frail boat. It was crushed into eternity.

David Bushnell made no such miscalculation, but he was a graduate of Yale College (it became a university in 1887). He had always been interested in the problems of submerged navigation; when the American War of Independence broke out in 1776, he saw the possibility of putting his work to useful purpose. The situation was simple. The British fleet was blockading the American colonies. Without any warships at their disposal, the colonists were unable to punch holes in this wall of oak, canvas, and cannon. According to Mr Bushnell's theory, the only way of fighting back was to build a secret weapon – something that could inflict damage out of all proportion to its size. Although he didn't use the word, Mr Bushnell proposed to build a submarine.

When it was completed, the strange vessel was named the *Turtle* – because, it was thought, it looked as if two turtle shells had been placed together. In fact, it bore a greater resemblance to an egg. Its hull was reinforced by a strong wooden beam across the middle, which also acted as a seat for the navigator. It was submerged by letting water into a tank at the bottom; brought to the surface

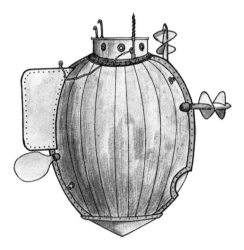

David Bushnell's *Turtle* made its appearance in the American War of Independence. It was an attempt to make the world's first combat submarine.

The idea was to bore a hole in the bottom of the enemy flagship and insert a charge of gunpowder.

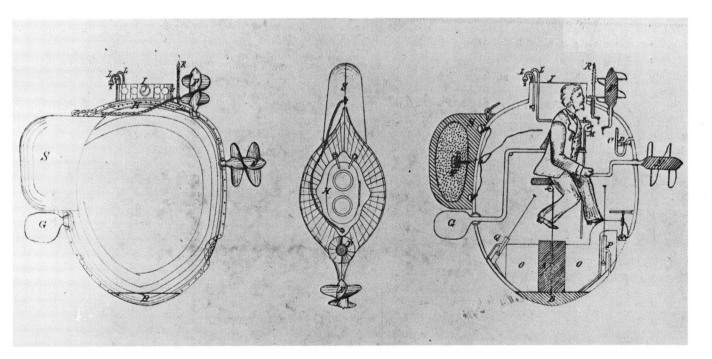

by pumping the water out. If this was not enough, there was 200 lb of lead ballast that could be jettisoned. There was enough air inside to keep the one-man crew alive for three hours.

On top of the hull, there was a brass conning tower – shaped rather like a top hat. Steering was by means of a rudder. A vertical screw enabled it to climb or descend when submerged; a horizontal screw propelled it through the water. There were also such navigational aids as a compass and a depth gauge (in fact, a barometer).

Mr Bushnell had rightly calculated that the most vulnerable part of a ship was its bottom. His plan was that the *Turtle* should be equipped with a charge of explosives carried on the outside of its hull. When it was in position, the vertical screw, rather like a drill, would be used to bore a hole in the enemy warship; the explosives would be inserted, and a clockwork timing device activated to give time for the *Turtle* to escape. Then, when the craft was safely out of range, a trigger would automatically fire a percussion cap.

Ideally, anyone who drove the *Turtle* should have had four hands; one to turn the handle that drove the horizontal screw, one for the vertical screw, one for the tiller, and another for such other tasks as releasing the explosives, working the pump, and so on. But, if he really extended himself, it was just possible for one man to do the work.

Bushnell's original intention had been for his brother to drive the *Turtle*. When the vessel was nearing completion, however, that gentleman became ill. The result was that the army was asked to provide three volunteers. Nobody, apparently, thought of adding 'seafaring experience' to the list of qualifications.

The first tests were carried out in Long Island Sound, and everybody agreed that they were promising. When in 1776 the British fleet was assembled off New York, the time had obviously come to subject the *Turtle* to her moment of truth. According to Bushnell, the first soldier chosen for the assignment was 'very ingenious and made himself master of the business'. Unfortunately he, too, fell sick. In the event, the mission was carried out by the second choice – a sergeant named Ezra Lee. The target was the 64-gun flagship of the British fleet, HMS *Eagle*.

Sometime during the night, Sergeant Lee and the *Turtle* were towed by a couple of rowing boats to within a few hundred yards of the warship. When the rope was cast off, the strong ebb tide swept the fledgling submarine beyond its objective. Lee had to remain passively at the controls until slack water; then he spent two hours toiling away at the screw until he was in position.

Nobody on board the flagship had noticed the strange intruder. Lee was able to submerge, edge up to the *Eagle*'s hull and get to work with the vertical screw. Unhappily, the underside of HMS *Eagle* was sheathed in copper. No matter how hard he turned the handle, the screw had no effect upon it.

Daylight was approaching, and Sergeant Lee decided that he had dallied for long enough. Safety lay four miles away; with the assistance of the tide, which was now on the flood, he might just about make it. There was a moment of doubt, as he passed Governor's Island. Two of the sentries noticed the *Turtle*'s brass conning tower bobbing about in the waves, and set out in a boat to investigate. Rightly deducing that the 150 lb of gunpowder were hampering his progress, Lee released them. The timing mechanism promptly came into action and, seconds later, the charge exploded. What with the blustery weather and the mystery of things that went bang in the night, the enemy returned to Governor's Island. Sergeant Lee came home safely.

There were no more attempts to use the *Turtle*. Nevertheless, Bushnell had succeeded in building a submarine that worked. Given a screw that could cut holes in copper, it might well have done substantial damage.

Robert Fulton was born in 1765 at Little Britain (now Fulton), Pennsylvania. He began his career as a jeweller's apprentice, and later became an artist. In 1794, he moved to England – where he worked with the Earl of Bridgwater on canal schemes. Presently he crossed the Channel and installed himself in the rue de Bac, Paris.

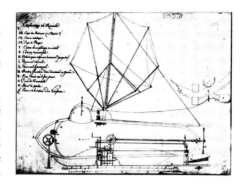

Fulton had many talents, but his greatest was as an inventor. Intellectually, he abhorred war; one of his gravest fears was that the United States might be compelled to squander its resources on a navy. As he saw it, the only way in which this could be avoided was by the construction of a device that would render all warships futile. The answer, he decided, was a submarine. Since the French ports were currently being blockaded by the English, the opportunities for experiment seemed to be prodigious.

On 13 December 1797, he wrote to the French Minister of Marine, outlining his ideas. He proposed to build a boat named the *Nautilus*. For every English ship of 40 guns or more it destroyed, he would be paid 4000 francs; for those of under 40 guns, 2000 francs. If, on the other hand, the *government* preferred to construct these submarines, he would be paid a royalty of 10,000 francs for every one completed.

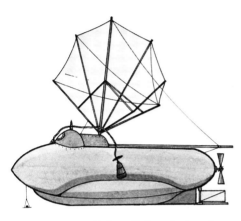

TOP AND ABOVE Robert Fulton designed his *Nautilus* with the notion of producing the ultimate weapon, something that would end naval warfare for all time. The *Nautilus* died from lack of support.

Such terms might have been acceptable, but Fulton's letter contained a clause that upset the minister. Fire-ships were regarded as against the rules of war. If they were captured, their crews were liable to be hanged. No doubt correctly, Fulton decided that a similar fate would be in store for captive submariners. With this in mind, his proposals insisted that they be given commissions; that, if taken into custody by the enemy, they should be treated as prisoners of war. If this were not done, the French should pledge themselves to take reprisals on English captives. Since there were three times as many Frenchmen languishing in English hulks as there were Englishmen in France, the minister turned the project down.

Three years went by, and Napoleon was installed as First Consul. Fulton produced his plan once more; this time, the response was more favourable. He was granted 10,000 francs for experimental work. The result was a boat 21 feet 4 inches long, with a conning tower at the forward end and inclined planes at the stern for stability. The hull was reinforced to withstand pressure at a depth of 25 feet. A mast and sail were provided for travelling on the surface – a hand-operated two-blade propeller took over for underwater journeys.

When the prototype *Nautilus* was completed in May 1801, it successfully carried out trials on the Seine – where it remained submerged for eight minutes. A few days later, Fulton and his boat moved to Brest. One or two modifications were carried out, such as replacing the candles used for illumination by scuttles (the former used up too much air). *Nautilus* was now ready to prove herself in the sea.

Again, she performed well. She even blew up an old schooner with a 20 lb charge of gunpowder. But if Fulton was expecting applause, he was to be disappointed. The crunch of the matter was the status of submarine crews in the articles of war. When the Minister of Marine was asked to finance a larger boat, he turned the request down. His conscience, he said, could not allow it. Even Napoleon now opposed him. On 5 February 1804, Fulton received what amounted to a letter of dismissal. Dejected, he moved to London. Perhaps the British government would be more receptive.

Pitt showed a flutter of interest, and appointed a commission to investigate the idea. The members rejected it. Admiral Earl St Vincent (First Lord of the Admiralty) described the Prime Minister as 'the greatest fool that ever existed to encourage a mode of warfare which those who commanded the seas did not want and which, if successful, would deprive them of it'. There was no more to be said. Robert Fulton returned to America, where he became more profitably engaged in the development of steamships.

ABOVE This submarine is an invention of a former German corporal, Wilhelm Bauer. To celebrate the coronation of Tsar Alexander II, Bauer has taken an orchestra beneath the waves to play the Russian national anthem.

BELOW Bauer's *Brandtaucher* made its first and last descent at Kiel harbour.

Nearly half a century later, the northern coast of Germany was under blockade by the Danish fleet. Once again, the mind of at least one ingenious character turned to the concept of submarines as the solution. In this case, it was a Bavarian artillery NCO, Corporal Wilhelm Bauer. In 1850, Corporal Bauer began work on his boat at Kiel. Named *Brandtaucher*, she was to be 26·5 feet long. Submersion was by means of flooding her double bottom; mechanical 'hands' were provided for the attachment of torpedoes to enemy ships. On 1 February 1851, Wilhelm Bauer was ready to demonstrate his vessel. At nine o'clock that morning, he was joined by two seamen and the *Brandtaucher* began her descent.

Corporal Bauer had blundered. At some point on the way down, the sheet iron that encased part of the hull crumpled. The boat settled uncomfortably in 54 feet of water – a hairline removed from absolute disaster. Work costing 13,800 francs had already been damaged beyond repair, and it seemed probable that three lives would shortly be added to the grim score.

When it came to calculating pressures and stresses, Wilhelm Bauer may have been inadequate. As a trapped submariner, however, he instinctively did the right thing. He let water into the submarine until the pressure inside equalled that on the outside. Then, as he had correctly foreseen, it became possible to open the hatches and escape. The *Brandtaucher* was a write-off; its inventor and his two companions shot safely to the surface.

But Bauer was discredited. In Germany nobody wanted to hear about his ideas. The Austrians showed momentary interest; a commission appointed by the emperor voted him 106,000 francs for experimental work – only to have its decision quashed by the Minister of Marine. In England, the Prince Consort introduced him to the shipbuilder William Scott-Russell – who characteristically stole some of his ideas, and then sent him packing. Bauer moved on to Russia, where he was more successful. Under the patronage of the Grand Duke Constantine, he built a boat named *Le Diable Marin*. It made its first descent on 6 September 1856. Since the day marked the coronation of Alexander II, a party of musicians went along as passengers. They played a no doubt nervous

rendering of the national anthem – after which the vessel surfaced. It was a fine demonstration, though not really what submarines are all about. According to some reports, *Le Diable Marin* submerged 135 times. Whatever the number, she eventually became stranded on a mudbank. Russia lost interest; like an underwater version of the Flying Dutchman, Corporal Wilhelm Bauer moved on to peddle his unwanted wares somewhere else.

The first submarine to sink a warship was a craft named the *H. L. Hunley* that, somewhat to their cost, the Confederates employed in the American Civil War. Once again, the cause of the *Hunley*'s creation was a blockade – in this case by the Federal States. Her inventor was a captain in the Confederate Army, Horace Hunley. His experiments had begun at New Orleans; when the port

Russian support of Bauer's submarine design efforts resulted in *Le Diable Marin*.

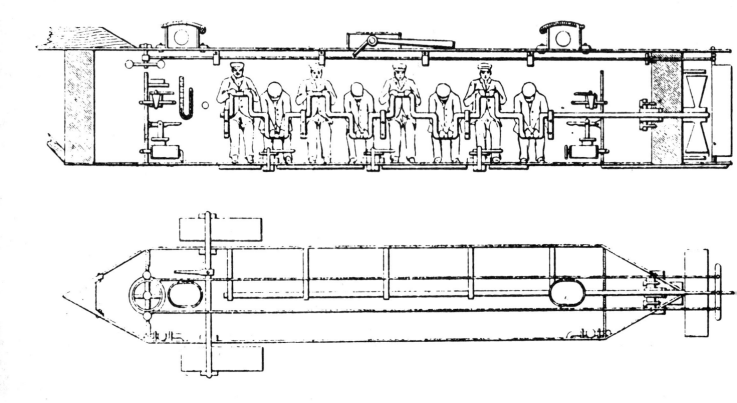

The confederate submarine *H. L. Hunley* was the first boat to sink an enemy warship. But the price was high: at one time or another, she killed almost everyone who sailed in her.

was occupied, he and his colleagues had to make a hurried journey overland to Mobile, Alabama.

Hunley's first idea had been to build a steam-driven submarine. He soon discovered, however, that there would not be enough oxygen available when the vessel was submerged. He toyed briefly with the notion of an electric motor; the principle was sound, but it was ahead of its time. All that remained was manpower. Eight men, sitting side by side, rotated a crankshaft that ran along the length of the vessel, and was connected to a screw at the rear. The helmsman sat up front, peering through a small conning tower. The weapon was a torpedo mounted on the end of a long spar jutting out from the prow.

If one is looking for an example of faith born out of despair, it would be hard to better the brief life story of the *H. L. Hunley*. In all, she made five journeys underwater, every one of them a disaster, at the cost of 32 lives; but it never occurred to anybody that the craft would be better scrapped.

On her first trial, she was commanded by a lieutenant named Paine. The boat was travelling on the surface with her hatches open, when a squall sprang up. The rising waves swamped the small craft; she filled with water and sank. Only Paine and one of his crew escaped.

On the next occasion, the *Hunley* capsized at her moorings. This time, the intrepid lieutenant and three men escaped. By this time, Paine had undergone enough misadventures. He returned to the safer profession of soldiering, and an officer from the 21st Alabama Infantry Regiment was sent to replace him. The newcomer did not survive for long. On the next trip, with Hunley himself on board, the boat foundered. There were no survivors. As a Confederate general noted when they hauled the *Hunley* to the surface: 'The spectacle was indescribably ghastly. The unfortunate men were contorted into all sorts of horrible attitudes, some clutching candles ... others lying in the bottom tightly grappled together, and the blackened faces of all presented the expression of their despair and agony.'

Pumped out and repaired, the *H. L. Hunley* sailed again. This time, she fouled the cable of a ship. Down she went; seven men were drowned. Since every

trip made by this submarine seemed doomed to disaster, it was decided that the time for trials was over. If she was to kill yet more men, she might as well take a fragment of Yankee shipping with her. The target was the USS *Housatonic*, one of the latest steam-driven warships.

At eight o'clock one night, the *Hunley* crept up on her unsuspecting prey in Charleston harbour. The torpedo was exploded just forward of the magazine, and the *Housatonic* settled quickly by the stern. Five of her crew were killed; the remainder were rescued by the boats of another man-of-war.

But the *Housatonic* did not die alone. Somehow, the little submarine had become wedged in the hole in the warship's side. As the pride of the Federal Navy plunged to the bottom, she took the *H. L. Hunley* with her. It was rather like a beast of prey dying with a parasite attached. It was also typical. To expect the *Hunley* to achieve greatness without also accomplishing her own destruction was to ask too much.

The 'Davids', also used by the Confederates, were powered by small steam engines. Hopefully, the tell-tale funnel would be mistaken for a plank of wood. It seems to have worked on occasion: at least two Federal warships were damaged by these midgets.

2 Emergent

The American Civil War was a laboratory in which new instruments of war were conceived, built, and tested – and sometimes found to be failures. The *H. L. Hunley* had shown that it was possible to destroy an enemy vessel from beneath the waves. It had also shown that, if such an art were to be advanced, something far better than the *H. L. Hunley* would be required. Indeed, the essentials of any submersible craft worth contemplating added up to a formidable list.

It would, for example, have to be capable of diving quickly – no matter whether it was stationary or moving. Under water, it must maintain an even depth line, and be able to contain enough fresh air to keep its crew alive and well. The hull needed to be strong enough to withstand considerable pressure; and large enough to contain a means of propulsion, ballast tanks, stores and weapons. There must also be a satisfactory method by which the submariner could control his direction, horizontally and vertically.

Nor was this all. Manpower as a means of submarine propulsion was clearly a last resort – just as the spar torpedo was an instrument of chance. There was no knowing whom it would kill, the intended victims or the men who wielded it. Much, clearly, had yet to be done.

By 1870, the solutions to some of these problems were already available. In 1866, Robert Whitehead had developed the propelled submarine torpedo. Its range was short and its speed slow, but it was a beginning. The electric motor had been invented; since it discharged no gases, it might have seemed to be the natural means of underwater propulsion. For the moment, however, people appeared to be obsessed by that apparent source of all nineteenth-century power and progress, the steam engine. One man who was particularly pre-occupied with its submarine potential was a Liverpool curate named George William Garrett.

During the late 1870s, one suspects that Garrett's flock suffered from neglect, such tasks as visiting the sick and attending Mothers' Union meetings yielding before a much greater undertaking. The Reverend George Garrett was inventing a submarine. The views of his vicar on the matter have not been recorded.

His first experiments produced a boat, 15 feet long and shaped roughly like an egg. Amidships was a small circular conning tower and hatch; water was pumped into ballast tanks in the bottom of the hull, and its single screw was rotated by turning a wheel. When it was tested in Liverpool docks, it worked well enough. Garrett was encouraged and applied himself to a much larger concept. The result appeared at the end of 1879.

The name of the boat was *Resurgam*. It was 45 feet long, equipped with hydroplanes, compressed air – and a steam engine. The idea was that you built up a huge head of steam before submerging. Everything was then sealed off and, with a bit of luck, the *Resurgam*'s stored-up power would be sufficient to drive her ten miles at a speed of two or three knots. The result was not entirely successful. On trials off the Welsh coast, she went down with a crew of three on board. Contrary to the promise implicit in her name, she did not rise again.

Such a vessel must have cost a good deal to build – far more, that is, than a curate's stipend would provide. Since Garrett left no account of his finances, we are left to wonder where the money came from. One possibility is that he approached that generous patron of needy inventors, the Swedish gunmaker Nordenfelt. The Swede was certainly aware of Garrett's work; and, despite the unhappy ending to the *Resurgam*'s story, he borrowed several of the clergyman's ideas. Being in the armaments business, he was also able to bring a more practical mind to bear on the question of weapons.

Nordenfelt first dismissed the spar torpedo as far too dangerous. Mines had not a great deal more to commend them: once a submarine had placed them in position, they could not be moved by her crew. On the other hand, it was

PREVIOUS PAGES The *Resurgam*, invented by a Liverpool clergyman, was powered by a steam engine. Contrary to the promise implicit in her name, she did not rise again when carrying out trials off the coast of Wales.

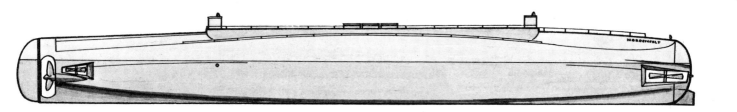

possible for the enemy to remove them. The more he thought about it, the more Whitehead's fishlike torpedo appealed to him. The usual vehicle for a torpedo attack was then a surface vessel named a torpedo boat, which was small, fast and exceedingly manoeuvrable. The difficulty was that, according to the current state of the art, the missiles could only be used at close range, and thus torpedo boats had to function by night. In daylight they stood a very fair chance of being shot to pieces. Working unseen beneath the surface, a vessel of stealth and secrecy, the submarine was a much more attractive proposition; if it needed the torpedo as an ideal weapon, the torpedo no less urgently needed the submarine.

Nordenfelt put his draughtsmen and engineers to work. Presently, in 1885, a submarine was produced in Stockholm. It was 64 feet long, displaced 60 tons, its steam engine gave it a range of 150 miles, and it was capable (or so Nordenfelt's men asserted) of diving to a depth of 50 feet. On 21 and 25 September 1885, it carried out trials before a distinguished gathering of Swedish society. On its first descent one of the hydroplanes was fouled by a ship's hawser. After the damage had been repaired, it went out again and spent six hours submerged. Throughout this period, a candle flickered cheerfully – showing that there was sufficient oxygen. It was certainly encouraging, but the candle's report on the atmosphere was inadequate. It gave no clue to the fact that there was a crack in one of the smoke boxes; and, through it, carbon monoxide was escaping. Some of the men on board became drowsy. One or two became unconscious. When they surfaced, they referred to the malady as 'smoke poisoning'. One of the crew was off sick for three weeks before he recovered.

On the whole, however, Nordenfelt was encouraged. The joints of the smoke box were strengthened, and the submarine was taken to the Solent off England for further trials. The *Nordenfelt I*, as it was called, was now modified to carry a Whitehead locomotive torpedo in an outside tube near the bow. As the shape of a possible man-of-war for the future, it impressed the Greek government sufficiently for it to purchase the boat for £9000. The Swedish arms magnate was now in business as a submarine producer.

For his next project, Nordenfelt sought the help of Vickers shipyard at Barrow-in-Furness, Lancashire. A 1300 horsepower engine was designed to give it a surface speed of 14 knots, or 20 miles at 5 knots underwater. This time, two torpedoes were contained in a pair of internal tubes, and a glass dome served as a conning tower. The boat was ready for the British naval review at Spithead in 1887. Among those who watched it with approval were representatives of the Tsar, who were quick to make Nordenfelt an offer. Unfortunately, they never received their purchase. The submarine was wrecked off Jutland on her journey to Russia.

The Turks, too, waved their chequebook at Nordenfelt. They wanted *two* submarines (presumably determined to go one better than the Russians). The contract was given to a firm on the River Thames at Chertsey. The boats were to be named the *Abdul Medjid* and the *Abdul Hamid*. In addition to carrying two 14-foot torpedoes, they were also to be armed with a pair of Nordenfelt

Nordenfelt's submarine was one of the first to be adapted to carry whitehead torpedoes.

machine-guns. When the first was completed, it turned out to be impossible to find a Turkish crew prepared to man her. Consequently, she set off for trials in the Sea of Marmora with Nordenfelt's English employees on board. The *Abdul Hamid* was left unfinished.

While that inventive parson, the Reverend Garrett, had been busy working out his ideas in Liverpool, other ingenious souls were exploring submarine possibilities in other parts of the world. A Russian named Drzewiecki produced a 16-foot boat in 1876. It was powered by pedals rather along the lines of a bicycle. The object was to attach bombs to the underside of an enemy vessel by means of rubber suckers. The Russian government ordered a couple, though it is hard to see why. A Spaniard, Isaac Peral, was much nearer the mark when, in September 1888, he unveiled a boat propelled by an electric motor. It was only 16·5 feet long and designed to be driven by a crew of two. In a sense, it was an extension of a much larger warship's armament, for it was intended to be carried towards combat on the deck of a battleship. And, back in Russia, Drzewiecki returned to his drawing-board – this time producing a version that, like Peral's, was equipped with an electric motor.

By the 1890s, it had become quite clear that the science of underwater navigation was emerging from the bizarre to the practical. It was clearly something that, sooner or later, would affect the fortunes of war at sea. The question to be answered was *when*? In 1896, in an attempt to speed the process of evolution, the French Minister of Marine announced a competition. Prizes would be awarded for the best submarine designs. The entrants could be of any nationality, but they had to observe certain stipulations. Whatever kind of boat was envisaged must be of no more than 200 tons displacement. It must have a cruising range of at least 100 miles – and a speed on the surface of 12 knots and 8 knots when submerged.

Predictably, the fertile mind of Drzewiecki got to work on the problem; and, no less foreseeably, his entry was his most ambitious effort yet. The projected vessel displaced 190 tons. Two torpedo tubes provided the armament; a steam engine gave it a surface speed (in theory, at any rate) of 15 knots. Underwater it was powered by an electric motor fed by an accumulator. It was awarded second prize out of 29 competitors.

The first prize winner was a Frenchman named Laubeuf, who put up an idea for a dual purpose vessel. Above the waves it was intended to function as a second-class torpedo boat and (as in Drzewiecki's design) was driven by a steam engine. In its submarine role an electric motor gave it a range of 25 miles at 8 knots (or 72 miles at 5 knots). It has been described as 'a submersible' as opposed to a 'purely submarine boat', but it contained one idea that was greatly to M. Laubeuf's credit. When it was on the surface, the steam engine was able to drive the electric motors in the manner of dynamos – and thereby recharge the accumulators. It may not have been the perfect solution to the submarine designer's dilemma of how to produce a sustained performance submerged. But it came very close to the answer.

Possibly the French minister felt he had received two vessels for the price of one gold medal. The winning entry was constructed at Cherbourg in 1897. Two years later, she was named the *Narval*, and, on one of her early voyages, she inflicted her first kill. The fact that it was unintentional did not seem to lessen its significance. When she was leaving harbour at a speed of five knots, she accidentally struck at right angles a tug named the *Navette*. The *Narval* suffered small damage from the encounter; but, as she went astern and withdrew, the tug promptly foundered. At once, the powers began to ask themselves whether a submarine need depend on torpedoes; might not these small vessels themselves become a lethal force – simply by ramming enemy warships?

The French navy had, in fact, taken possession of its first submarine eight years previously. The boat was a 60-foot affair named the *Gymnote* – powered by a 55 horsepower electric motor assisted by 564 accumulators. It was used only experimentally, and the experiments never amounted to much. On paper, she may have been attractive – in practice, she never handled with that instant obedience, that apparent awareness of her element, that makes all the difference between a good idea and an exercise in mediocrity.

At about the time when pioneer French submariners were groping in the depths around Toulon in the *Gymnote*, there was an outburst of indignation in the corridors of naval power at Paris. The Germans had built two vessels of the Nordenfelt type – one of them at Kiel, the other at Danzig. Both were the work of a French designer named d'Equevilley. There was a nasty smell of treason about the business; a feeling that, before long, M. d'Equevilley would be taken severely to task for selling secrets to France's time-honoured enemy. In fact, as an investigation soon revealed, M. d'Equevilley had already offered his ideas to the French government and had been turned down. Nor was he in fact doing his country any great disservice by retailing them to the Germans. The boats were not very good ones.

In America, the authorities were watching the development of submarines in Europe with increasing interest. The US Navy Appropriation Bill for 1893–4 listed $200,000 to be spent on this new type of vessel. For the moment, however, there was no suitable claimant for the expenditure. Somehow, the imaginations of inventors must be stirred up. As in France, a competition for designs was chosen as the method.

Advertisements were published in the leading newspapers. Competitors were recommended to bear in mind eight vital points. Whatever they submitted must

The French submarine *Gymnote* was powered by an electric motor and ought to have marked an important step forward. But when she was employed experimentally off Toulon in 1888, she did not handle well. Nevertheless, she suggested that, given certain modifications, it was possible to maintain a steady course when submerged.

be safe, be easy to submerge and reliable under water, have a reasonable speed on the surface and under it, have a sturdy endurance above and below the waves, be suitable for offensive operations, be stable and, finally, provide a clear view of the target. Out of all the entries, three seemed to merit more serious attention.

The first of the trio was known as the Baker Boat. It was sent in by the Chicago-Detroit Dry Dock Company. The hull, shaped like a cigar, was to be built from six-inch seasoned oak and would, its designer assured, withstand a pressure of 75 pounds per square inch. It was equipped with electric motors and steam engines (also to be used for charging the batteries); ventilation was provided by two tubes reaching up to the surface. Electric fans were employed to suck air down them. The boat was built and put to the test with two men on board. She remained submerged for one hour and forty-five minutes. In terms of speed she was adequate, but it was impossible to maintain an even depth line.

The second entry (and this order does not suggest the outcome of the contest) was from an Irish immigrant teacher named John Philip Holland. He had been interested in submarine navigation ever since his first job at a school in County Cork. In 1875, he had designed a one-man boat in which the crewman propelled himself by bicycle pedals and wore a diver's helmet. His inspiration on the occasion of the competition came from the Whitehead torpedo. In the notes accompanying his entry, he wrote:

'The submarine boat is a small ship on the model of the Whitehead torpedo, subject to none of its limitations, improving on all its special qualities, except speed for which it substitutes incomparably greater endurance. It is not, like other small vessels, compelled to select for its antagonist a vessel of about its own or inferior power; the larger and more powerful its mark, the better its opportunity.'

You may say that these are pretty substantial claims, but Mr Holland had worked hard on his project – it was, indeed, his seventh attempt to produce a workable submarine, and the competition adjudicators were impressed by his ideas. On 13 March 1895, the US Navy offered him a contract to turn them into reality. Mr Holland's response was immediate. He formed the Holland Boat Company in New Jersey; on 23 June of the following year the keel of his dream boat was laid. She was to be named *Plunger*.

When the *Plunger* was completed, she measured 85 feet long, and had a surface displacement of 140 tons. Two sets of triple expansion steam engines, using gasoline as fuel, provided the power for two propellers. On the surface, they pushed her along at 14 knots. When she was submerged, however, they revealed an uncomfortable flaw. Whatever the good qualities of the *Plunger* may have been, her machinery made the interior intolerably hot.

There was no point in suggesting that J. P. Holland should go back to his drawing-board – he was already at it. Aware of the *Plunger*'s faults, he was designing (and building at his own expense) a successor. The newcomer was smaller – only 53 feet long and displacing 75 tons on the surface. But the important thing about her was the motive power. In place of the steam engine, an Otto gas engine was used. Underwater she cruised at 5·5 knots; on the surface at 7. What was more, the gas engines provided a convenient means of charging her batteries. Holland had not produced the definitive submarine, but he was only a few yards away from it. The US government rewarded his efforts with a payment of $120,000 and the recommendation that it be used by the navy.

The third short-listed competitor was a man named Simon Lake. At a quick glance his entry looked as if it had been run up in a back yard. Fourteen feet long and constructed from yellow pine, it bore more resemblance to a chest than a boat. It is very difficult to be serious about Mr Lake; for although no

Submarine pioneers

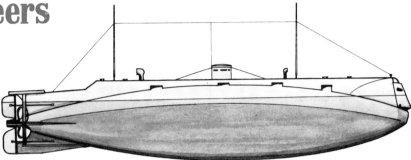

ABOVE the breakthrough in submarine design was the invention of John P. Holland. The *Plunger* (above right) was Holland's first dream.

BELOW Simon Lake in his laboratory at Milford, Connecticut, in 1939.

BELOW RIGHT Holland's boat was powered by an electric motor and an internal combustion engine.

doubt a dedicated submarine designer, he was by nature an advertising man. His assertions were fantastic, his demonstrations extravagant, and his ideas showed a desperate striving after originality. While eveyone else was thinking about propellers as the logical method of underwater propulsion, Mr Lake seemed determined to be different. He mounted his boat on wheels – intending it to be driven on the seabed much like a car. The fact that the floor of the ocean might be littered with rocks, that there might be hills and crevices just as there are on land, does not seem to have occurred to him. The navy took a more realistic view and rejected his submission. But this did not deter the resolute Simon Lake. He simply got down to it and built another, more ambitious version.

Lake might have done better if he had read the rules of the contest more carefully. The US government was looking for an underwater warship. Simon Lake, on the other hand, was experimenting with craft more suited to salvage work. There were ingenious air lock devices by

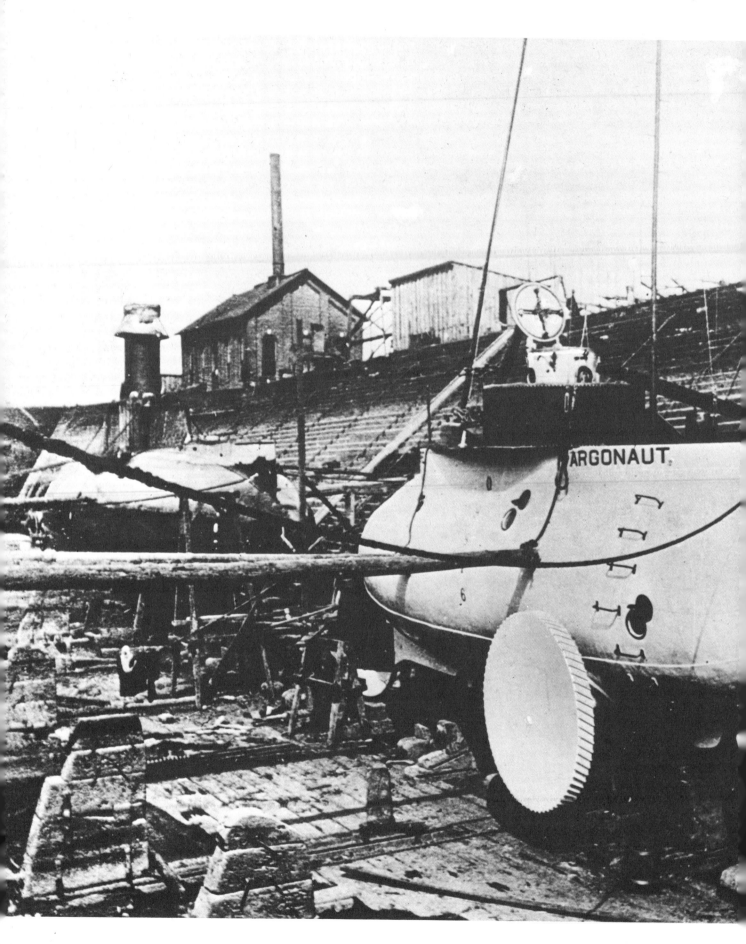

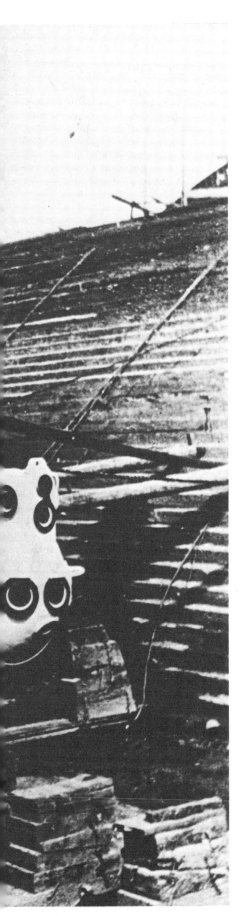

which men clad in divers outfits might enter and leave the vessel underwater. No doubt, to misquote a French general, they were magnificent, but they were not war.

A glance at Holland's efforts might have encouraged Lake to revise his ideas, but he seemed determined to continue as he had begun. The wheels became larger; a metal hull replaced the wooden version; more effective power was provided – in the shape of a gasoline engine (it drove the wheels and, for surface cruising, a propeller); refinements such as an enormous searchlight were included; and so on. But the US authorities remained unimpressed. When his self-estimated masterpiece, *Argonaut*, was produced in 1897, he celebrated the occasion by inviting members of the press for a trip. Champagne was served and, or so the story goes, they were permitted to leave the boat and gather clams from the seabed.

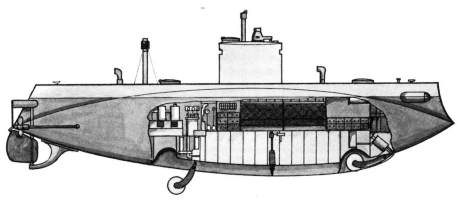

He may not have been honoured in his own country, but the hopefully prophetic Lake was not without small successes elsewhere. His boat the *Protector* bore a closer resemblance to the emerging shape of submarines, though it was still equipped with wheels. In an attempt to sell it to the Russians, he explained that it would be ideal for such tasks as cutting cables and destroying mines. He must have been convincing, for the Tsar's naval authority ordered four. They were built at Newport News Shipbuilding and Dry Dock Company at Newport News, Va.

By now, the US Navy was becoming mildly interested in the enterprising Simon Lake. When he had approached it in 1901, he had been politely advised to go away and study the Holland approach. By the time the *Protector* came off the slipway it could be seen that at last he had tried to compromise. One of its features was a spacious conning tower. Inevitably, there were wheels – but these amounted to little more than the artist's signature. For much of the time they folded up into the hull like an aircraft's undercarriage. At least it was worth studying. The board appointed for the examination was sufficiently impressed to recommend the purchase of five. They were to be used for the protection of the entrances to Chesapeake Bay, Long Island Sound, San Francisco Harbour, and Puget Sound. The fifth was to be set aside for training purposes.

Holland's efforts had brought him prestige but little else. This extremely intelligent schoolmaster-turned-inventor had arrived in the United States penniless. Now, despite contributions from the United States government, he was again desperately hard up. Had it not been for a considerable injection of cash from a well-wisher with a shrewd eye for the future of naval warfare, his work might have come to an end. As it was, it became possible to found the Electric Boat Company. In 1900, this firm sold the United States Navy its first submarine. The cost was $150,000. Fifty-five years later, the same undertaking produced the USN's first nuclear-powered submarine. This time, the price was $30 million – and that did not include the propulsion machinery.

PREVIOUS PAGES:
RIGHT Lake's *Protector* bore the closest resemblance to what was becoming the accepted shape of submarines.

LEFT Lake's earlier efforts were nothing if not original. Wheels were intended to carry them across the ocean bed in much the manner of land vehicles. Behind the *Argonaut* is John P. Holland's more practical *Plunger* of 1898.

By 1900, the British Admiralty had become aware of Holland's achievements, and was searching its heart for an attitude to this new instrument of war. Opinions were mixed. When Fulton offered his *Nautilus* to the government all those years ago, the *Naval Chronicle* pounced on the ideas as 'revolting to every noble principle'. Fulton was condemned as a 'crafty murderous ruffian', and his boat as one of 'such detestable machines, that promised destruction to maritime establishments'. Now, at the beginning of the twentieth century, the attitude remained in some quarters. Admiral of the Fleet Sir Arthur Wilson made no secret of his abhorrence. With passionate invective, he described it as 'underhand, unfair, and damned un-English'.

By contrast Lord Fisher, soon to become First Sea Lord, was full of enthusiasm. 'The submarine', he wrote in a memorandum, 'must revolutionise naval tactics for this simple reason – that the present battle formation of ships in a single line presents a target of such a length that the chances are altogether in favour of the Whitehead torpedo hitting some ship in the line . . .' He enjoined:

'Imagine even one Submarine Boat with a flock of transports in sight loaded each with two or three thousand troops! Imagine the effect of one such transport going to the bottom in a few seconds with its living freight!

'Even the bare thought makes invasion impossible! Fancy 100,000 helpless, huddled up troops afloat in frightened transports with these invisible demons known to be near.

'Death near – momentarily – sudden – awful – invisible – unavoidable! Nothing conceivable more demoralising.'

Britannia had managed to rule the waves without assistance from forces beneath them. That situation, in Lord Fisher's opinion, was now past. A Holland-type submarine was bought from America. In 1902, after the design

The Royal Navy's first submarine was dubbed the *A1*. It was lost in 1904 after being rammed by a liner.

had been modified, five such boats were ordered from Vickers at Barrow. The first was named, without very much originality, *A1*. Completed in 1904, she displaced 180 tons. A Wolseley gasoline engine gave her a surface speed of 11 knots; her electric motors propelled her at 8 knots when submerged. Although she and her early companions were bedevilled by engine trouble, she was considered to be a great improvement on the Holland boat. Not the least of her interesting features was a periscope. It had been invented by a young torpedo specialist, Captain R. H. S. Bacon – working in collaboration with a Dublin optician.

But despite the enthusiasm of Fisher, the majority of naval officers continued to view the eccentric newcomers with suspicion. They were good only for defending harbours; and even worse, they represented a threat to battleships. Next to the reigning monarch, those cumbersome grey giants were closest to the average naval officer's heart. There was something furtive about a submarine – as if it were a skulking sneak thief of the ocean. A battleship meant prestige.

In Berlin, too, opinions were divided. When HMS *Dreadnought*, the greatest battleship of her day, was completed in 1906, Germany became aware of a threat that was underscored by Lord Fisher's certainty of an eventual war between Britain and Germany. The obvious answer would be to build Dreadnoughts for the German navy; but for the moment there was a snag. Until the Kiel Canal was widened in 1914, it was impossible for these huge ships to make a quick passage to Wilhelmshaven and Brunsbüttel – Germany's two harbours on the North Sea. The answer seemed to be to invest in a large force of torpedo boats and submarines. But, it was asked, were the latter really necessary? The water off the German coastline was shallow. What, then, could possibly be the purpose of a submarine? Not the least of the doubters was Grand Admiral Alfred von Tirpitz, who has been described as 'the creator of the German navy'.

Nevertheless, and despite the relatively poor performance of d'Equevilley's boats, the engineers at Krupp's Germaniawerft plant in Kiel were working on the idea. In August 1905, a boat 116 feet 8 inches long was launched. Her 200 horsepower internal combustion engine gave her a surface speed of 11 knots; her electric motors propelled her at 9 knots when submerged. She had a range of 1000 miles, she could dive in five minutes, she was equipped with twin periscopes – and a gyroscopic compass made accurate underwater navigation possible.

The boat was built at Krupp's own expense. At about the same time, however, an order was on its way from the government. It was for a similar vessel, and it was to be called *das Unterseebooteins* (the *U1*). Like the British, the Germans failed to climb the heights of inspiration when it came to naming their underwater fleet.

One way and another, the shape of the submarine was almost complete. But there was still a flaw in the design – the use of petrol engines. Since gasoline is a highly volatile spirit, there was an ever–present risk of explosion. The *A5* was destroyed in this way on 16 February 1905, after she had completed refuelling.[1]

Prudently, the German Admiralty had shown its mistrust at the very outset. When the *U1* was built she was fitted with a heavy oil engine. By the time *U19* was laid down in 1911, the diesel engine was far enough advanced, and she was equipped with two of them. This was the breakthrough that submarine designers had been waiting for. Not only had diesel oil a lower flash-point than petrol (and was therefore safer), it was also less ready to evaporate. Consequently it was more economical.

The grand design of submarines was now complete – at any rate for the time being. In Germany, Britain and France, the pieces for the war game were ready. It required only one or another power to make the first move. There was no need to be impatient. It would come soon enough.

3 Warlike

ABOVE A model of Bushnell's *Turtle* as it appeared at a submarine exhibition at the National Maritime Museum, Greenwich, in 1976 – two hundred years after its inception.

OPPOSITE ABOVE An impression of an early submarine design attributed to Kopechy.

OPPOSITE BELOW An illustration from A. Robida's *La Guerre au Vingtième Siècle*, published in Paris in 1887, depicting a midget and a full-size submarine.

O n 2 September 1914, *U21* of the Imperial German Navy lay on the surface recharging her batteries. Her position was off May Island, an empty lozenge of land at the entrance to the Firth of Forth in Scotland. The past few days had been eventful ones for her commanding officer, Lieut-Cdr Hersing, and his crew of 38. On 1 September, in company with *U20*, they had managed to penetrate the firth. Hersing had gazed through the periscope at the gaunt, grey shape of the Forth Bridge that carried the railway north of Edinburgh; with greater intensity, he had studied warships lying at anchor off the naval dockyard at Rosyth. The time might come when they could steal into the heart of such an assembly, creating havoc and destruction. But such a time had not yet come. Like thieves in the night, the *U21* and the *U20* withdrew to open water.

By noon on the second, the weather had worsened. A heavy swell was running, making conditions aboard the *U21* uncomfortable. Suddenly, a look-out directed Hersing's attention to a ship that had appeared some distance ahead of them. They could just make out a lean grey hull and three spindly smoke stacks. The vessel was clearly a British light cruiser. Hersing gave the order to dive.

A German U-boat.

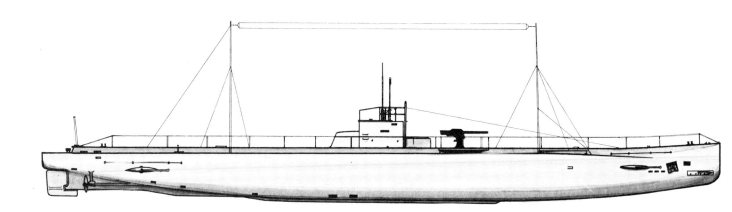

PREVIOUS PAGES By the time the German *U15* (seen here on passage through the Kiel canal) was completed in 1912, a submarine equipped with diesel engines was under construction. The *U15* was lost in 1914 when HMS *Birmingham* rammed her off Fair Isle, north of Scotland.

The cruiser was moving quickly; it was impossible to get within torpedo range, and Hersing called off the attack. *U21* surfaced once more and resumed the charging of her batteries. The weather was now worse than ever. At 3.45 pm, the cruiser re-appeared. Again, Hersing ordered his men to dive. This time, there was no problem concerning range. The *U21* was able to sneak up on her unsuspecting prey unseen. The distance gradually closed. Hersing, his eyes peering through the periscope, ordered one torpedo to be fired. The seconds ticked away until it seemed that it must have missed. Then it happened: an explosion from a point just abaft the cruiser's bridge. A cloud of smoke enveloped the forepart of the vessel as, slowly, her stern rose out of the sea. Within four minutes, she had sunk. Two hundred and fifty-nine men out of her complement of 296 went with her. HMS *Pathfinder* had become the first man-of-war to be sunk by a submarine since the affair of the *H. L. Hunley* and the *Housatonic*. Even if she had been aware of the *U21*, it is doubtful whether she could have done much about it. In 1914, the only action a surface vessel could take against a submerged submarine was to ram her. That, too, might have been the end of HMS *Pathfinder*.

Although there was no deadline in the evolution of the submarine, it was a strange circumstance of history that it was ready in time to become one of the most formidable naval weapons in the First World War. Indeed, so far as Germany was concerned, it became *the* weapon – though nobody could have

predicted this during those uncertain days of 1914. It was one of those instances in which the minds of the inventors had moved more rapidly than those of the admirals. The truth is that the latter had no idea of the submarine's potential – or of how to use it. The supreme commander of the German navy, Admiral von Tirpitz, was sceptical about them. Despite the enthusiasm of a now ageing Lord Fisher and his ebullient First Lord, Winston Churchill, a similar mood prevailed in the chambers of Whitehall. On paper, the odds of whatever underwater battles were to come seemed to favour Britain. The nation had a total of 74 boats against Germany's 33. But this was misleading. Eleven of the British belonged to the A class, which had been obsolete for some time; none, with the exception of eight D class vessels (the first in Britain to be equipped with diesel engines) and a handful of Es were capable of working more than a short distance from the UK coast. Churchill had been eager to build a fleet of ocean-going submarines; but, he sadly observed, 'great technical difficulties were encountered, and the delays of the contractors and of the Admiralty departments were vexatious in the extreme'.[2]

By contrast, the German U-boats were nearly all ocean-going vessels, and they were soon to prove their capability. Indeed, one of the advertisers in the 1914 edition of that British bible of naval might, *Jane's Fighting Ships*, was none other than Krupp's Germaniawerft. The illustration featured a submarine built by the firm for Italy; the copy concentrated on export successes. Were they ready to replace the 'contractors' who had given Churchill so much cause for complaint?

ABOVE The ship was a tanker, bringing vital supplies of oil to Britain during the First World War. Somewhere beneath the waves there is a U-boat whose torpedo has delivered the thrust of death.

In the control room of a First World War
German U-boat; painting by Felix
Schwormstädt.

During the following four years, the German Submarine Service proved to be a far greater destructive force than the British. But this was understandable, for the latter suffered from lack of targets. The occasions when one submarine sank another were rare, and usually happened by accident. As for surface ships, as Churchill wrote,

'Except for a few sudden dashes to sea by fast vessels, the occasional unexpected voyage of a single cruiser, or a carefully prepared, elaborately protected, swiftly executed parade of the High Sea Fleet, the German Navy remained locked in its torpedo-proof harbours; and outside of the Baltic all German commerce was at an end. On the other hand, every sea was crowded with British merchant craft – dozens of large vessels arriving and departing every day . . .'

It would have been interesting to see what might have happened at the Battle of Jutland, if a sizeable force of submarines had been let loose among the surface giants. But such a thing would have been impossible. Even on top of the water, these boats would have found it difficult to keep up with the rest of the pack; submerged, it would have been impossible. Few of them could cruise at more than nine knots on their electric motors – and then only for short periods. If the power in their batteries were to last for any length of time, a more realistic speed was about two knots.

OPPOSITE ABOVE The Royal Navy's *A11* was completed by Vicker's shipyard in 1905, but by the time war was declared she was obsolete.

OPPOSITE BELOW Britain's 'D' class submarines were the first to employ diesel engines. The *D2* was completed in 1910 and, shortly afterwards, Winston Churchill, the First Lord of the Admiralty, made a trip in her from Portsmouth.

The interior of a German U-boat under construction, showing the engine compartment. The conditions were horribly cramped, but the boats were reasonably cheap and could be mass produced.

Meeting on the high seas, First World
War. In the foreground is the periscope of
an English submarine that just missed
sighting the German U-boat; painting by
Claus Bergen, 1917.

The first evidence that a submarine might be superior in range and endurance to the notions entertained by both the British and German Admiralties was provided by Lieut-Cdr Hersing. Some weeks before his *U21* had made history by sinking the *Pathfinder* – before, indeed, war had broken out – he set sail from Heligoland for a ten-day patrol between Stavanger and the Firth of Forth. The fact that he not only completed his assignment, but also covered 1500 miles, gave even Tirpitz cause for thought. It was the longest sustained voyage hitherto accomplished by a submersible boat, and made a nonsense of the commonly held idea that such vessels would have to put into port every two or three days.

Although the British Admiralty held the submarine in low regard, the fleet commanders were uncomfortably aware of the threat this unseen presence posed to warships in harbour. A report of two U-boats lurking in the Pentland Firth off the north of Scotland caused the Grand Fleet to depart in unseemly haste from its anchorage in Scapa Flow. The alarm turned out to be unnecessary; but, had he known the identity of one of the U-boat commanders, the C-in-C, Admiral Jellicoe, might have had even more cause for concern. The officer in question was a dashing character named Otto Weddigen, the first of the much acclaimed (within Germany, at any rate) U-boat heroes.

Lieutenant Weddigen had first distinguished himself on 12 September 1914, when he was patrolling off the coast of Holland. His instructions were to pose the maximum threat to British troop transports on passage to Ostend. Throughout the previous day, the weather had been so bad that, during the

The elderly British cruiser, HMS *Aboukir*, was one of a trio sunk by Otto Weddigen off the coast of Holland on 12 September 1914. She foundered twenty-five minutes after the torpedo struck her.

evening, he dived his boat (the *U9*) to spend the night in the calmer waters below. Next morning, he surfaced to recharge the batteries. The weather was still rough.

The *U9* had not been on the surface for long when a cloud of smoke, penetrated by masts, appeared on the horizon. As they came closer, Weddigen could make out three cruisers steaming abreast at a speed of about 10 knots. Each was separated from the others by two miles. Despite the fact that his batteries were still low, Weddigen gave the order to dive. At 6.20 am, he ordered the first torpedo to be fired. It hit the central cruiser, which began to list heavily. Within 25 minutes, she had capsized and sunk.

Weddigen's victim was an elderly man-of-war named HMS *Aboukir*. She had been patrolling the region of the Dogger Bank in company with her sisters *Cressy* and *Hogue* to support the operations of destroyers working from Harwich. On the seventeenth, the weather had become so atrocious that the smaller ships had been compelled to return to port. The cruiser trio were now on their own. Known as 'the live bait squadron', the ships were, perhaps, expendable. The 1400 officers and ratings on board were not.

Throughout their patrol, the cruisers had seen no signs of any submarines. When the *Aboukir* was rent by an explosion and sank, the commanding officers of the *Cressy* and *Hogue* assumed that she had struck a mine. They closed in and began rescue operations.

Hogue was the next to go. Two torpedoes struck her ancient hull; she sank within ten minutes. A glimpse of the *U9*'s periscope suddenly made *Cressy*'s captain aware of what had occurred. Ordering the engine-room to coax every fragment of speed from the machinery, and with the cruiser's four funnels belching black smoke, he tried to make a run for it. It was too late. At 7.17 am, his batteries now almost flat, Weddigen fired two more torpedoes. HMS *Cressy* rolled over on to her beam ends. Fifteen minutes later, she joined her sisters at the bottom. *U9* headed homewards.

On 13 October, the *U9* reappeared in the Pentland Firth; she dispatched the ancient (built in 1893) 7700-ton cruiser HMS *Hawke*, and caused the wave of anxiety that sent Jellicoe and his fleet hurrying seawards from Scapa. But Weddigen's life as an intrepid submariner was almost over. In early 1915, now commanding the *U29*, he sank a ship off the south coast of Ireland. By this time, the Straits of Dover had been closed to German warships by means of drifting nets. After one U-boat had become entangled in them, the German Admiralty decided that they represented too great a hazard. All German submarines were instructed to return to their bases via the north of Scotland.

Lieutenant Weddigen and the *U29* were back again in the now familiar waters of the Pentland Firth. The date was 18 March; the submarine was just emerging into the North Sea when, by one of those remarkable accidents of chance, she came across the Grand Fleet at exercise. She was spotted by the battleship HMS *Dreadnought* – flying the flag of Vice-Admiral Doveton Sturdee, commander of the Fourth Battle Squadron. Sturdee gave orders to ram. It took ten minutes for the giant warship to round on its quarry and to crunch through her slender hull. *U29* sank with all hands. In Britain it was felt that the loss of *Aboukir*, *Hogue* and *Cressy* had been avenged. In Germany there was mourning for the death of a hero. Lieutenant Weddigen had been awarded the Pour le Mérite (the Blue Max – Germany's highest military decoration). He was the first U-boat commander to receive it.

Germany's field of submarine warfare may have been wider than Britain's, but the Royal Navy was not hanging back. Had the captain of the *D6* been more fortunate, he – and not Hersing – could have taken credit for the war's first kill. He was on patrol off Heligoland, when the SMS *Bostock* steamed into sight. With a flat calm and clear visibility, the conditions were ideal. The *D6* managed to stalk up to within 500 yards of her intended victim. When a pair of torpedoes

Otto Weddigen was the first U-boat commander to receive Germany's top award for valour, the Blue Max. He died when his *U29* was sunk with all hands by HMS *Dreadnought*

LEST WE FORGET

FAC-SIMILE OF MEDAL STRUCK BY GERMANY
TO COMMEMORATE THE EVENT
Translation of wording on Medal

BUSINESS ABOVE EVERYTHING	NO CONTRABAND – THE
CUNARD LINE – CUNARD-BOOKING	GREAT LINER LUSITANIA
OFFICE – SUBMARINE DANGER	SUNK BY A GERMAN SUBMARINE
	5TH MAY 1915.

The Sinking of the Lusitania.
May 7th 1915.

ABOVE The sinking of the *Lusitania* was commemorated in many British homes by this poster. The Kaiser, who later had cause to regret the work of his over-zealous submarine commanders, declared a public holiday to celebrate the event. A medal (bottom left) was struck bearing the words: 'Business above everything Cunard line – booking office – submarine danger'; and on the other side: 'No contraband – the great liner *Lusitania* sunk by a German submarine – 5 May 1915.' In view of the wording it is not surprising that only fifty were distributed in Germany. On the other hand, British Naval Intelligence got hold of the design and minted thirty thousand.

OPPOSITE:
ABOVE A german U-boat takes the crew of a sunken merchant ship aboard; painting by Felix Schwormstädt, 1917.

BELOW LEFT One side of a medal issued to commemorate Bauer's achievements in submarine design.

BELOW RIGHT First World War U-boat poster.

was fired, they ran straight for the target. But there was no explosion. Owing to a defect, they passed underneath.

Shortly afterwards, Lieut. Max Horton (later Admiral Sir Max Horton, who won fame for his anti-submarine successes in the Second World War) did better, when he dispatched the 2040-ton *Hela* to the bottom. A few days later, he also accounted for the destroyer *S116*. But, so far as the North Sea was concerned, a sinking by a British submarine was a rare event. The sorry fact was that there were not enough vessels to sustain a continuous blockade of Heligoland Bight – the strip of water leading to Wilhelmshaven and, by way of the canal, to Kiel. Instead, it was carried out at long range by surface craft patrolling the entrance to the English Channel, the Straits of Dover, and by a cruiser screen stretching from the north of Scotland to Iceland. In the Baltic, however, the British submariners were faring better.

The main object of submarine operations in these waters was to inhibit the export of iron ore from Sweden to Germany. The greater part of the force assigned to it were E-boats. The first of this noble class, the *E1*, was completed in 1913. With five torpedo tubes, a 12-pounder gun, and a very passable turn of speed, *E1* and her companions represented the cream of the British Submarine Service's vessels. Indeed, so far as underwater operations were concerned, they bore the brunt of the war. The only snag, and this was by no means peculiar to them, was the range of their wireless telegraph: it was far too short.

Once a submarine was out of radio contact, the only means of communication was by carrier pigeon. It was a poor substitute. On one occasion, the captain of an E-class boat on patrol off Heligoland needed to send an urgent message to his depot ship at Harwich. At 4 am he ordered four pigeons to be dispatched – each of them carrying identical words. Their owners' traps lay about 140 miles away in a west-south-westerly direction; the wind was moderate.

Presently, the birds came home. Their owners then had to remove the slips of paper and take them to their nearest post offices, where the contents were telegraphed to the Admiralty. The Admiralty decoded the cryptogram, noted the contents, and put it back into cipher once more. Then they transmitted it to the depot ship, where it had to be decoded all over again. An urgent communication that had left the submarine all those hours ago eventually reached its destination at three-thirty in the afternoon. It was all very well unless you happened to be in a hurry.

But the inadequacy of their radios was not the only problem to plague the British submariners in the Baltic. Another was the fact that they were put under the command of a Russian admiral. His own crews were backward and inefficient; he himself was a difficult man to get on with. Nevertheless, despite all

An example of a British 'E' class submarine, used primarily in the First World War.

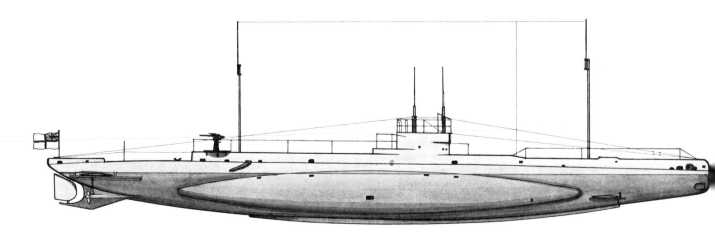

this, the submariners helped themselves to substantial pickings. In October 1914, the *E9* commanded by Lieut-Cdr Cromie returned from patrol after accounting for six ships, carrying a total of 20,000 tons of ore. Eventually, after further sinkings, the trade had to be suspended until a force of German warships could be assembled to protect the merchantmen. It amounted to two cruisers and a flotilla of destroyers. In October of 1915 the *E8* sent the cruiser *Prinz Adalbert* to the bottom; one month later, the *E19* sank the *Undine*. Then the Baltic froze over for the winter, and operations came to a halt.

The British submarines in the Baltic deserved a better fate. When the Bolsheviks signed a peace treaty with Germany in 1918, eight of them sailed out of Helsinki in forlorn procession. Presently, in 15 fathoms of water, they blew themselves up using their own torpedo warheads. The gallant Lieut-Cdr Cromie eventually made his way to St Petersburg (now Leningrad), where he was cut to pieces by a mob trying to invade the British Embassy.

If the word 'Baltic' was carved with pride on the hearts of the First World War British submarine crews, it was certainly not allowed to obscure the exploits in the Dardanelles. Of the two, these were the more spectacular, indeed, sufficiently so that no fewer than four of the personnel involved were to be awarded the Victoria Cross. The first boat to make the perilous passage along the straits leading to the Sea of Marmora was the *B11* commanded by the youthful Lieut. Norman Holbrook. Completed in 1906 and equipped with a petrol engine and two torpedo tubes, the *B11* had no business to be in such hazardous waters. It would have been more appropriate if she had been stationed somewhere at home – guarding, perhaps, the entrance to a port.

The British submarine *B11*, built in 1906, was obsolete when she went into action in the Sea of Marmora. Even so, she managed to sink the Turkish battleship *Messoudieh* (inset).

When Turkey aligned herself with the Central Powers on 31 October 1914, the *B11* was keeping a distant watch on the Dardanelles in company with two other obsolete British submarines and four equally ancient French ones. The more succulent prizes to be won or sunk from the new enemy lay in the Sea of Marmora, 35 miles distant up a narrow, heavily-mined and -fortified channel. Unless the Turkish commanders decided to come westwards and fight, it seemed they would remain unmolested for the whole of the war. Nothing – above all, not a vessel of such ancient build and uncertain performance as the *B11* – would be able to penetrate this lethal gutter into their lair.

But the commanding officers of the Allied submarine force found the work of watch-dogs dull. If only to relieve the monotony of gazing across an expanse of usually sunlit water, they were eager to pit their skills and their hapless craft against the Dardanelles. The opportunity came when reports reached the commander of this mixed flotilla that Turkish ships were lying halfway up the straits at Chanak. This made a difference; the submarines could now make a bid for glory. *B11* was selected for the operation – largely because she was the only ship in a fit condition even to attempt such an undertaking.

The *B11* returns in triumph after her exploit in the Sea of Marmora. On her way back, her compass ceased to function and she grounded several times. After eight hours, she reached safety, and applause.

Lieutenant Holbrook and his crew of 15 set off after dark. It took them five hours, skirmishing with a complexity of currents and passing underneath five rows of mines, to reach Chanak. Once there, however, they found a delectable target in the shape of a massive elderly *grande dame* of a Turkish battleship named the *Messoudieh*. Lieut. Holbrook took careful aim; he then discharged a torpedo which, with astounding accuracy, plunged into the *Messoudieh*'s side. The effect was immediate. One moment, Chanak had been swathed in nocturnal silence; the next, every gun for miles around seemed to be shooting at the *B11*.

The voyage back was a nightmare such as only a submariner can truly understand. The batteries were drained almost to the point of exhaustion. The submarine's compass gave trouble, producing wild and senseless directions as if to prove that it, too, was a stranger to this dreadful place. On several occasions the *B11* ran aground; and, whenever her periscope peeped up, there was more firing from either shore. Eventually, after eight hours, the *B11* returned to her flotilla. The operation had been nobly executed.

Lieutenant-Commander E. C. Boyle in *E14* made the full trip to the Sea of Marmora – spending 21 days there. Among his victims was a large transport bound for Gallipoli with 6000 troops and a battery of field-guns on board. When he had run out of torpedoes, Boyle was ordered to remain on patrol. The very presence of the *E14* was, it seems, enough to cause confusion among Turkish shipping. In an attempt to disguise the fact that his entire armament was now reduced to a rifle, he used an oil drum, a length of pipe and a piece of canvas to rig up a dummy gun.

Eventually the *E14* was relieved by the *E11* commanded by Lieut-Cdr Martin Nasmith. During a 19-day patrol, Nasmith accounted for a Turkish gunboat, three transports, an ammunition ship and three store ships. The American consul at Constantinople reported that 'the Marmora is practically closed by English submarines'. General Sir Ian Hamilton, the army's C-in-C at Gallipoli, was heard to remark that one submarine was 'worth an army corps'.

Britain and Germany were both producing a new type of hero: a man who went about his business in dark waters, continually exposed to danger, living under impossibly uncomfortable conditions, and dependent on quick thinking and shrewd judgement to compensate for unreliable instruments. In 15 years, the boats themselves had come a long way from such basic essays in submarine design as the Hollands. Between them, the men and the vessels were achieving deeds worthy of stories in adventure magazines such as *The Boys' Own Paper* (and, of course, its German equivalent). But even now the submarine had not revealed the true measure of its power. The tales told in this chapter have a kind of innocence about them that was not to survive for long. Before 1915 was very old, the submarine would become entangled by politics – and before the war was over, it would reduce at least one of the protagonists to a condition not far removed from starvation.

4 Unrestricted

In the year of Our Lord 1512, King Henry VIII of England produced a code of conduct for the treatment of enemy merchant ships upon the high seas. Known as the Cruiser Rules, the articles instructed that any warship encountering an unarmed vessel should halt her by firing a shot across her bows. A boarding party would then carry out a search. If the ship belonged to a neutral country, she must be allowed to continue her voyage. If she was hostile, the crew and passengers were to be taken as hostages – the vessel and the freight as prizes. If, however, the encounter took place too far from a friendly port, or if there were not enough men to provide a prize crew, the ship and the cargo might be destroyed. The Cruiser Rules, it should be emphasized, applied only to *unarmed* merchantmen travelling without an escort.

For over three hundred years, King Henry's instructions to his Admiral of the Fleet had been unquestioned by the powers which eventually adopted them. Now, with the coming of the submarine, they were studied again. For several years, Lord Fisher had made no secret of his belief that these boats might be used to sink merchant shipping. Winston Churchill had disagreed with him. Writing to Fisher on 1 January 1914, he observed, 'There are a few points on which I am not convinced. Of these, the greatest is the question of the use of submarines to sink merchant vessels. I do not believe this would ever be done by a civilized power.' It was presumably the privilege of the First Lord of the Admiralty to change his mind. Before the year was out, Churchill was ordering a flotilla of British submarines to the Baltic – with instructions to intercept merchantmen carrying iron ore. Since there was no room on board for prize crews, it was inevitable that the vessels would be sunk. In other matters, or so it is said, the commanding officers scrupulously observed the Cruiser Rules.

The attitude of German submariners varied. When, for example, Lieut-Cdr Feldkircher of the *U17* sank the steamer *Glitra*, outward bound from Grangemouth to Stavanger, his conduct was beyond reproach. The *Glitra*'s master was given ten minutes in which to abandon ship. Once the merchantman had been sunk by opening her sea-cocks, the *U17* took the lifeboats in tow until they were within a reasonable distance of the Norwegian coast. Similarly, Lieut-Cdr Hersing was a model of correctness. On patrol off the coast of Lancashire, he came inshore to bombard a cluster of airship sheds near Barrow-in-Furness. Shortly afterwards, he stopped and scuttled three merchant ships. In each case, the crew was given plenty of time in which to escape. Hersing even instructed some fishing boats in the vicinity to help with the rescue.

Lieutenant-Commander Schneider was an altogether tougher proposition. Six days after Feldkircher's sinking of the *Glitra*, he came across the French steamer *Admiral Ganteaume* in the Channel. He torpedoed her without warning. As it happened, the vessel was carrying 2500 Belgian refugees. There was immediate panic, and 40 lives were lost. However, before Schneider is condemned out-of-hand, it should be remembered that the English Channel was a very different place from an isolated patch of ocean off Norway. The sea abounded in British patrol boats of one kind or another. The German submariner was taking no chances. Indeed, Schneider was one of the more courageous and tenacious of the U-boat commanders. On 31 December 1914, he came across eight pre-Dreadnought battleships carrying out gunnery practice off Portland. At dusk, they turned up Channel towards the Isle of Wight – with, unknown to them, Schneider's *U24* trailing along behind. The barometer was now falling; the sea was choppy.

At one o'clock on the following morning, the *U24* sighted them again – this time, to the north. The U-boat closed until she was within 700 yards of HMS *Formidable*. Then Schneider fired his first torpedo. It missed.

One and a half hours later, the *Formidable* was again silhouetted against the night sky. Schneider sent off a second torpedo, which struck the ageing battleship amidships. The boiler-room was flooded; the giant swung out of line with a

PREVIOUS PAGES U-boats operated relentlessly against British shipping in both world wars.

severe list. Presently all the lights went out. Schneider waited 45 minutes, then fired a second torpedo. This, too, smashed into the target. For a few moments, it seemed as if the second hit had somehow put *Formidable* back on to an even keel. Then it could be seen that she was sinking by the head. At 4.45 am, she slid under the water. Of the 780 officers and men on board, 547 were drowned. So far as the Royal Navy was concerned, it was an unhappy beginning to 1915.

Nobody could question the ethics of HMS *Formidable*'s sinking. It was, after all, a case of one warship in combat with another – even though the odds were a good deal less than even. But they could, and did, say some harsh things when – also in January 1915 – Lieut-Cdr Schwieger, the newly appointed commanding officer of *U20*, torpedoed three vessels in the Channel without warning – and when, two days later, he sank the 12,000-ton hospital ship *Asturias*. There could be no question of mistaken identity, for the former liner was painted white and the red crosses on her sides were illuminated.

In the early days of the war, Grand Admiral Tirpitz had gone on a visit of inspection to the Krupp Germaniawerft shipyard at Kiel. When he saw the lines of submarines under construction, he remarked: 'Well, you know, these

The *U24* was completed at Danzig Dockyard in 1913. Armed with 4 torpedo tubes and a 3.4 inch gun, she survived the war. In 1918 she was handed over to the Royal Navy and was scrapped in 1922.

are going to be much too late for this war.' It was typical of a commonly held belief that the hostilities would not continue for very much longer.

But the German land offensive ran out of thrust. The armies became bogged down in the useless slaughter of trench warfare – a condition that wrought a terrible price in terms of human lives, but which did not advance the cause of either side one inch. Simultaneously, the British blockade of Germany from the sea was beginning to bite. The only expedient left to the Kaiser and his government was to force the United Kingdom into starvation. The submarines being built at Kiel would not be too late for the war. They and their sisters already in service would become the instrument of this strategy.

On 4 February 1915, the German government issued what might have been construed as an ominous warning. According to the declaration,

'All the waters surrounding Great Britain and Ireland, including the whole of the English Channel, are hereby declared to be a war zone. From 18 February onwards every enemy merchant vessel found within this war zone will be destroyed without its always being possible to avoid danger to the crews and passengers.

'Neutral ships will also be exposed to danger in the war zone, and in view of the misuse of neutral flags ordered on 31 January by the British Government, and owing to unforeseen incidents to which naval warfare is liable, it is impossible to avoid attacks being made on neutral ships in mistake for those of the enemy.'

The use of neutral flags was excused by Churchill, who pointed out that it was 'a time-honoured naval stratagem [we had authorized] knowing well the embarrassment it would cause to the enemy submarines'. For the rest, the document, while not exactly pulverizing the Cruiser Rules, was a clear implication that they would be respected only when it was convenient.

Eleven days after the declaration had been published, the Kaiser summoned his Chief of Naval Staff. If unrestricted submarine warfare were carried out, could he compel the British to surrender in six weeks? The Kaiser obviously wanted the answer to be 'yes'; the officer, Admiral Bachmann, meekly nodded his head. Yes, he said, it was possible.

In fact, the first phase of unrestricted submarine warfare did not cause any marked discomfort to Britain. The U-boat blockade began on 18 February; by the end of the first week, out of the 1381 vessels that arrived at or departed from UK ports, only 11 were attacked, and only 7 sunk. During the second week, out of 1474 arrivals and departures, only three came under fire from U-boats and all of them escaped. By the end of the month, trade to and from the British Isles was proceeding very much as usual. The truth was that there were not yet sufficient U-boats to make the campaign effective. According to one estimate, no fewer than five of these submarines were needed for each station. Of this total, one would be ready for combat, another would be on her way home, a third would be on her way to relieve the first, a fourth would be undergoing repairs in dry dock, and the fifth would be preparing for sea. Since the German submarine fleet at this time numbered only about one hundred – and this included the small UB series designed for coastal work, and the UC-boats which were small minelayers – and since the ocean was very large indeed, the force had to be thinly scattered.

But if the U-boats' harvest was small, it was nevertheless spectacular. It made an impact on the mind of the world, producing the kind of publicity that the Germans could well have done without. In early May 1915, the *U20* commanded by Lieut-Cdr Walter Schwieger was on patrol at the southern approaches to the Irish Sea. When, on 6 May, the Harrison liner *Candidate* was sunk, the operation was carried out in strict accordance with the Cruiser Rules. During the search, however, Schwieger's men discovered that she was carrying two machine-guns and a six-pounder. The rules, it will be remembered, applied only to *unarmed* merchant ships. The result was that when, not long afterwards, the *Candidate*'s sister ship *Centurion* appeared, she was torpedoed without warning.

After that, fog put a stop to the *U20*'s activities. In any case, there were now only three torpedoes left. Schwieger intended to conserve two for any targets that presented themselves on the voyage back to Germany. At last, on the morning of 7 May, the fog lifted. At 1.20 pm, the *U20* was lying on the surface, recharging her batteries and preparing to go home. At this instant, a look-out reported a smudge of smoke on the horizon. Presently the shape of a steamer with four funnels, about 14 miles away, became apparent. Schwieger gave the order to dive. Almost simultaneously, he passed on the details of his observations to the navigating officer. The latter had no hesitation in identifying the ship as either the *Lusitania* or the *Mauretania*.

It was almost as if the liner's captain was determined to fall into the *U20*'s trap. At 2.35 pm, he ordered a change of course to starboard that, as Schwieger noted in his diary, 'makes possible a drawing near for firing'. The submarine closed on the doomed ship at full speed. At ten minutes past three, he fired a torpedo at a range of 700 metres. It struck the target at a point just abaft the bridge. The *Lusitania*, for it was she, sank with the appalling toll of 1,198 men, women and children. Many of them were citizens of the United States.

The rights and wrongs of the *Lusitania* affair have been argued interminably. The generally held belief that Schwieger put two torpedoes into her is belied by the evidence of the U-boat commander's own log. Undoubtedly a second explosion occurred, and it was this that finally destroyed the great Cunarder. But it was more likely caused by a consignment of contraband explosives on board (they appeared in the cargo manifest as 'cheese' and 'furs', but there is everything to suggest that this document was inaccurate). The German press protested that the liner 'was heavily armed. She was an auxiliary cruiser.' When the British government contributed to the building of the *Lusitania* in 1903, the Admiralty had conceived just such a wartime role for her. There were, indeed, provisions for mounting guns on board. But eventually the idea had been dropped; at the time of her sinking, she was carrying no armament at all.

Many years were to elapse before the facts about the *Lusitania*'s contraband cargo became public. Lieut-Cdr Schwieger certainly did not know about it. Nor could he have seen any evidence of a gun, for there was none. Perhaps his experience with the *Candidate* had made him wary, but this is a thin excuse. His only justification, if he had any at all, was that a profile of the *Lusitania* was printed in the 1914 edition of *Jane's Fighting Ships* – a copy of which was certainly on board the *U20*, just as it was among the reference books in almost every other warship.

The sinking of the *Lusitania* has been apocryphally given as the reason why the United States declared war on Germany. Since nearly two years elapsed between the first event and the second, this verdict is far too bland. It makes a comfortable conclusion to the anecdote, but that is all one can say. More truthfully, it was the beginning of a chain of events that produced this conclusion. In every instance, the cause was the unthinking (or over-zealous, depending on your point of view) action of a U-boat commander.

On 19 August 1915, the White Star liner *Arabic* was about 60 miles to the south of Queenstown (now Cobh), Ireland, on passage to New York. On board were 181 passengers and a crew of 248. Also on the spot were Lieut-Cdr Schneider and his *U24*. Although the *Arabic* was clearly a passenger steamer, Schneider did not hesitate. With no warning, he plunged a torpedo into her side. The *Arabic* sank within ten minutes; but, by a magnificent feat of seamanship and impeccable discipline, all but 44 of the liner's population got away in the boats. The anger that the loss of the *Lusitania* had begun in America became greater

The DEATHLESS STORY of the LUSITANIA

England will not forget those who have died in her cause

By GERARD FIENNES

The leviathan's death-blow.

ON Friday, May 7th, the Cunard steamship, Lusitania, bound from New York to Liverpool with just under two thousand souls on board, was torpedoed without warning off the Old Head of Kinsale by a German submarine or submarines, and sank in about twenty minutes. Seven hundred of her passengers and crew were landed at Queenstown and Kinsale, of whom about fifty were dead or dying. The rest are missing.

Such a plain statement of fact would be sufficient to arouse the horror and indignation of the whole world. No possible excuse or explanation could suffice to wash from the hands of the Kaiser and von Tirpitz the damned spot which doth "the multitudinous seas incarnadine." But let the tale be told from the beginning.

On May 1st the Lusitania left New York, having on board of her a company which included British, Americans, Dutch, Scandinavians, Italians, Greeks, Spaniards, Persians even. Almost every neutral nation in the world was represented, and all were civilians travelling upon their lawful occasions of business and pleasure. Among them, Mr. G. A. Vanderbilt, millionaire and sportsman; Mr. Charles Frohmann, the well-known theatrical manager; Mr. D. A. Thomas, M.P., and his daughter, Lady Mackworth; Sir Hugh Lane, Lady Allan, and many others notable in various ways. Among them was an unusual number of children, many of them babies in arms.

Before the ship sailed, the extraordinary advertisement printed on this page appeared in the American Press.

This "formal" notice was followed by anonymous messages sent to persons intending to travel in the Lusitania, warning them not to embark in her. The Germans said, "We did it to ease our conscience, lest harm should come to persons uninformed." But the recipients laughed at the warnings, when they did not curse their impudence, and the great ship steamed proudly out of New York harbour, the Blue Ensign floating over her taffrail.

The internal plot had been well and truly laid. The Lusitania was a prize particularly desired of the Germans for many reasons. She represented the successful effort of the British to recover the "blue riband of the Atlantic" from Herr Ballin. When the Morgan Combine was formed twelve or thirteen years ago, and other British lines passed under American control (which was to a great extent German), the British Government advanced over two millions and a-half to the Cunard Company on easy terms to build two ships which should be the largest and fastest crossing the Atlantic, and should, under all circumstances, remain wholly British. The Lusitania and Mauretania were built to Admiralty specifications, of exceptional strength of scantling, to steam twenty-five knots, and to be at the disposal of the Admiralty as reserve cruisers when they should be required. It is noteworthy, and to be noted, in view of the sequel, that, while the Admiralty have taken up a number of ships, P. & O., Orient, White Star, and other Cunarders, including the latest and biggest, the Aquitania, they did not take up these two ships on which they had a special lien. The Lusitania, though nine years old, still held the "blue riband," and there is no doubt that Herr Ballin, who deeply resented the fact that the British Government subsidised her construction, used all his influence to have her out of the way when peace shall once more, if ever, restore the normal competition.

After a fortnight's comparative quiescence in the pirate campaign, during which the officers of the "U" boats apparently confined themselves to sinking neutrals and British trawlers

Facsimile of Huns' warning as it appeared in American newspapers.

3

than ever; the correspondence between Washington and Berlin took on an even sharper tone. Indeed, the Kaiser became so worried that, on 27 August, he issued an order that passenger steamers must receive adequate warning – and could only be sunk if there were no danger to the passengers.

Matters came to a head on 24 March 1916, when the small coastal submarine *UB29* was operating in the area off Dover. When the cross-channel steamer *Sussex* appeared at the approaches to Folkestone harbour, the commander, Lieut. Pustkuchen, torpedoed her without any warning. Although the packet boat managed to limp into port, 50 of those on board were killed by the explosion. Among them were women and children – and Americans. This was the last straw. In an angry editorial, the *New York Herald* wanted to know 'How many more Americans must be killed before Wilson declares war?'

President Wilson reacted quickly. In a harshly-worded note to the German Chancellor, he wrote, 'Unless the Imperial German Government shall now immediately declare and carry into effect its abandonment of the present method of warfare against passenger and freight carrying vessels, the Government have no choice but sever diplomatic relations with the German Government altogether.'

That did it! Admiral Scheer, the commander of the High Seas Fleet, called his U-boats back to harbour. To their profit, there had been the sinking of 0·25 million tons of shipping; to their loss an appalling effect on relations with the United States.

During the next few months, the Atlantic did, in fact, witness the crossing of at least two German boats. Possibly in an attempt to break the British blockade, or perhaps as a public relations gesture, eight German submarines were ordered as mercantile cruisers. They were exceptionally large and well capable of crossing the Atlantic. One of them, the *Deutschland*, twice made the

OPPOSITE This account of the sinking of the *Lusitania* was published in a magazine, *War Budget*, on 22 May 1915. Before the great Cunarder sailed from New York, the Germans published a warning to travellers in the American press; it was reprinted at the foot of this article.

ABOVE When a U-boat torpedoed the cross-channel steamer *Sussex* on 24 March 1916, her captain claimed he had mistaken the passenger ship for a cruiser. The cartoonist of the Philadelphia *Record* was sceptical, especially as several Americans had been killed by the explosion.

BELOW Captain Paul König and his crew of the German submarine, *Deutschland*. Travelling under the flag of the North German Lloyd shipping company, the *Deutschland* crossed the Atlantic from Kiel to Baltimore, acting as a merchant vessel. After two trips, the venture was abandoned.

passage from Kiel to Baltimore, sailing under the flag of the North German Lloyd shipping company. On the outward trip, she carried dyes and precious stones; on the return voyage, she was loaded with such commodities as zinc, rubber, copper and nickel. On the second journey she was escorted by the *U53*, a conventional submarine with her ballast tanks modified to carry extra fuel. Unfortunately, the *U53*'s captain could not resist the harvest of temptation that lay just outside US territorial waters. Before he set course eastwards, he had accounted for three British merchant ships, one Norwegian and one Dutch. Another mercantile submarine, the *Bremen*, also set out for America, but she never arrived.[3] The remaining vessels were converted into warships, and became the *Us 151–7*.

Submarine warfare in the North Atlantic had, apart from the depredations of *U53*, been halted. In the Mediterranean, however, it continued to flourish. This was the realm of the greatest U-boat ace – certainly of the First World War, possibly of both. He was Lieut-Cdr von Arnauald de la Perière. The latter part of his name came from a French ancestor who, in the eighteenth century, fell out with the Duke of Bourbon and served under Frederick the Great. Significantly, the German Official Naval History always refers to him as plain von Arnauald.

In a manner of speaking, this officer was an artist in the destruction of vessels. He seemed to be able to smell opportunity – just as his nostrils were no less sensitive to the scent of danger. On one patrol in the Aegean lasting 24 days, he sank 90,150 tons of Allied shipping. It was a record that has never been beaten. His total score for the war was 400,000 tons. Von Arnauald never made a mistake, and he never transgressed the Cruiser Rules. Indeed, his methods of attack seldom varied. When he was 5000 yards from his quarry, he fired a warning shot. Once the ship had been abandoned, he closed to 2000 yards to finish the victim off. As in the case of many U-boat commanders, he preferred to carry out the sinking by gunfire, conserving his torpedoes for bigger or more dangerous game.

If American public opinion had largely been responsible for the lull in the North Atlantic blockade, German popular opinion must take some of the responsibility for its resumption. On the home front, the citizens had become fed up with a diet of turnips and similar hardships occasioned by British action against overseas trade. At a higher level, Hindenburg and Ludendorff, who were running the army, were complaining that there could be no successes on the Western Front unless unrestricted U-boat warfare were resumed. The Chancellor, Bethmann-Hollweg, was opposed to the idea. Germany had troubles enough without incurring any more wrath from the United States. In the end, a kind of compromise was produced. First of all Germany would offer to negotiate peace terms, preferably through American mediation. If this approach failed – if, so to speak, the country was *compelled* to go on fighting – an all-out submarine campaign would be sanctioned. The negotiations failed; on the evening of 8 January 1916, the Kaiser decided to send the U-boats back into action. On the following morning, he informed Bethmann-Hollweg of his decision. Whatever the Chancellor's reservations may have been, the rest of Germany was delighted. Even the Stock Exchange sent a telegram of congratulations. Previously, the Chief of Naval Staff had promised that the war would be over in six weeks. Now there was greater realism. The time allowed for the reduction of Great Britain was set at six months.

On this occasion it was a very different story. If the Battle of Jutland had proved anything, it had shown by its very indecisiveness that the outcomes of wars do not depend upon the clash of giant fleets. Afterwards, as if preparing for this new endeavour, the entire emphasis of German naval construction was devoted to U-boats. Surface ships even received cuts in their crews to swell the ranks of the submarine service. By the time the new blockade began, there

were more than enough vessels for the task. Indeed, at one time, it looked as if six months might be a conservative estimate.

In January alone, 181 vessels totalling 298,000 tons were sunk. In February, 468,000 tons (259 ships) were destroyed – and so it went on, rising relentlessly month by month, as the British winter began to transform itself into what promised to be a very sombre and hungry spring. The German Admiralty estimated that it was possible to maintain sinkings at the rate of 0·5-million tons a month. In fact, they underrated themselves. When the April figures were published, they showed the horrifying figure of 849,000 tons.

According to Allied propaganda, the average U-boat crew was a bunch of psychopathic killers intent on starving to death innocent women and children. Somewhere in mid-Atlantic, the Cruiser Rules had been ditched. Now the submariners struck without warning – killed, it appeared, without compassion. In fact, most German seamen were just like many other young men in the fighting services of either side. They were sometimes afraid, sometimes excited, and nearly always damnably uncomfortable. At about this time, the Americans referred to their vessels as the 'pig boats'. The description might have been applied to the species as a whole. The toilet arrangements were rudimentary; supplies of fresh water were limited; there was no refrigeration (if the diesel engine represented one break-through in submarine evolution, the production of canned goods represented another). Even when the boat was submerged, it was hard for the off-duty watch to get enough sleep. In what should have been the still of the deep, there was an almost ceaseless racket. Torpedoes were being moved; repairs were being carried out on the engines; or else there was that character who seems to haunt so many ships – a man you never actually see, but who appears to divide his time between shuffling lengths of chain and clanking one piece of metal against another.

Under such conditions, the only thing that kept a man going was success. For the time being, there was plenty of it. Even at home, the authorities did their best to squeeze the most out of it. U-boat crews were heroes – that was official. They were garlanded with laurels, adorned with iron crosses, and given very special treatment wherever they went.

This giant of 1,875 tons (submerged) was originally built as the mercantile submarine *Oldenburg*. Towards the end of the war she was armed with two 5·9 inch guns and a pair of torpedo tubes, and renamed *U151*.

During the First World War, American submarines were nicknamed 'pig boats'. But the squalor caused by cramped accommodation and inadequate washing facilities was common to all boats, no matter what their nationality.

Out at sea, these men sank ships without fear – and, unfortunately for their employers, with little discrimination. One out of every four British merchant ships that left port never returned. The proportion for neutral shipping may not have been quite so high, but it was substantial enough. Finally the United States lost patience. There had been enough protests, sufficient warnings. On 6 April 1917, President Wilson declared war on Germany.

America had much to offer the Allied cause, but submarines were not among the items. The USN's boats were mostly short range coastal craft incapable of crossing the Atlantic under their own power. Nevertheless, that was where they had to be – there was no point in hoping that German targets would obligingly present themselves off the eastern seaboard. Somehow, then, they must be helped across, and the only way of doing this seemed to be to tow them.

As anyone who has tried to take a submarine in tow will tell you, the task is fraught with problems. Moving a floating dock across an ocean is simple by comparison. However, a flotilla of K-boats, numbered 1 to 8 inclusive, set off for the Mediterranean by this method. On the way, they were caught by a storm, with the result that only *K1*, *K2*, *K5* and *K8* survived to reach the Azores. Wisely, perhaps, they remained there for the rest of the war – working as patrol craft out of Ponta Delgada. Their loss so far as operations in the Mediterranean were concerned cannot have been great. Even a K-boat's most ardent admirer (and there were not many) had to admit that they were not very wonderful.

The L class boats were certainly better; but they, too, set off for Ireland under tow. Once again, a storm barred their passage. The warps were cast off and, with more hope than optimism, the submariners were told to go it alone. To their credit, they all succeeded in reaching Berehaven in Bantry Bay. Thereafter, they were employed on anti-submarine patrols. There were one or two sightings, but no kills.

Meanwhile the U-boat stranglehold on Britain had to be prised loose. By December 1916, a form of depth charge had been produced, but there were nothing like enough to go round. The only method of dealing with a submerged submarine, unless it happened to strike a mine, was to ram it.

But since weapons were not the answer to the problem of the blockade, some new strategy had to be devised. The search for ideas need not have put a severe strain on the Admiralty's intellectual capacity. Strangely enough, the method already existed.

Ever since the outbreak of war, troopships had travelled in convoy. The system had worked wonderfully well. Why, then, might it not be applied to merchantmen? If they were grouped together instead of strung out, they would be harder to locate. They could be protected by escorts of destroyers, and they could be diverted from danger spots by radio. The troopship convoys had been completely immune from attack. Surely this success could be repeated?

The idea was greeted by opposition from almost every direction. If a U-boat penetrated such a cluster of shipping, the results would be beyond imagining. Assembling convoys would create dreadful delays. The speed of passage would be slowed down, since they would have to travel at the rate of the most laggardly member. There were not enough destroyers for the task. The destroyers were required for other operations . . . and so it went on. The only people who seemed to have any faith in the notion were a group of young staff officers at the Admiralty – and the Government. Even master mariners professed to be against it.

Eventually, Lloyd George, the prime minister, put his foot down. On 10 May 1917, the first merchant ship convoy sailed from Gibraltar. On 4 June, regular convoys were introduced to and from the USA; on 20 June they were extended to Canada; and, on 31 July, the first South America-bound convoy departed.

In the event, there were more than sufficient escorts. Indeed, the solution could not have come at a better time; for, on the North Atlantic run, twenty-five per cent of the destroyers were provided by the US Navy. At the same time, the development and production of depth charges was proceeding quickly, and new methods of detecting submarines were being fitted to men-of-war. Suddenly, the toll of U-boat sinkings dramatically fell off. Robbed of success, the morale of their crews went into a sharp decline. Somehow it seemed the German submarine service had lost its heart. The fatigue, the hardship and now the danger – these all became too much. A matter of months had transformed an instrument that might have won the war into a collection of rusty boats manned by prematurely old young men. By now there was reason for them to feel old. The average U-boat crew could expect to make only six voyages before being wiped out.

One of the last attacks was made by von Arnauald, when he sank a straggler from a ten-ship convoy off Cape Finisterre. When he reached Kiel on 14 November, he found that the port was in the hands of mutineers, and that red flags were flying from the warships' masts. Handing over to his First Lieutenant, von Arnauald changed into civilian clothes and went quietly ashore. It was a sad homecoming for a great warrior.

But if the seeds of the future are planted in the past, the most significant event took place on 4 October. A U-boat was engaged in attacking a convoy in the Mediterranean when she went out of control. With considerable skill, her commanding officer managed to surface the vessel – only to be met by a devastating barrage of fire from a cruiser and a small pack of destroyers. The boat had to be abandoned; the chief engineer and six hands went down with her, and the captain was one of those taken prisoner. For the next several months, he languished in a British prisoner-of-war camp. He spent most of the time pondering on U-boat warfare – considering the mistakes, analysing the successes, and wondering how it might have been done better. In years to come, he would have plenty of opportunities to put his ideas to the test. The man's name was Karl Doenitz.

His experts had promised the Kaiser that U-boat warfare would starve England in six weeks; the period was amended to six months. Both estimates were wrong, as a cartoon in the *New York Herald* pointed out.

5 Uncertain

Had the invention of the submarine been of any value to mankind? There had always been doubters and, at the end of 1918, they must surely have felt vindicated. During the previous four years, this new engine of war had accounted for 14,820,000 tons of shipping – 354,450 tons of it belonging to the United States. This grotesque feat of destruction had been accomplished by not many boats, reasonably cheaply produced, and manned by seldom more than 40 sailors apiece. The number of U-boats lost is uncertain. One estimate puts the number at 404, but this assumed that 975 were in operation – which is rubbish. Two hundred and three is a more likely conjecture. If added to the 128 handed over to the Allies after the Armistice, the total becomes reasonable.

The condition on which the victorious powers claimed their shares of the U-boat fleet was that the vessels must eventually be destroyed. They could study them; carry out trials, if they liked; but the ultimate destination had to be the scrap-yard. In Britain, it seems doubtful that this scrutiny was put to very

PREVIOUS PAGES For surface attacks the crews of U-boats relied on their guns. The armament of most of their vessels was made up of 4·1 inch guns and four torpedo tubes.

BELOW 'H' and 'L' class boats at that stronghold of British might, Fort Blockhouse, Portsmouth.

much purpose. There were still high ranking naval officers who were sceptical about the submarine's future. It had admittedly shown its value as a commerce raider. But this must never be permitted to occur again. In any case, having produced successful E and (latterly) H-boats, the country was engrossed in another flight of inventive fancy. Once again, it sprang from uncertainty about the submarine's true role in warfare; an unwillingness to accept it as a kind of corsair – a determination to regard it an integral part of the fleet.

In 1915, Admiral Jellicoe had visualized submarines as units in the Grand Fleet. Once the surface vessels had become engaged in battle, they would leave the main formations and cut off the enemy's retreat. The trouble was that there was no vessel in existence which, even travelling at full speed on the surface, would be able to reach the scene in time to be useful. In an attempt to create the type of boat Jellicoe wanted the K class was devised. Instead of being powered by diesel engines, these ships were equipped with steam turbines. They were almost double the length of the average submarine, and on the surface they could

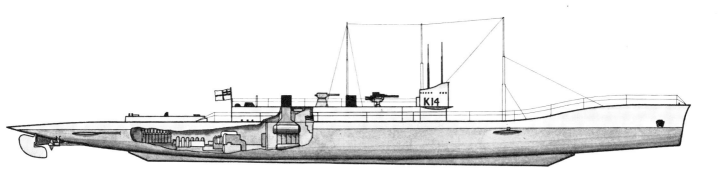

reach 25 knots when their machinery was really pressed. Submerged, their electric motors could manage no more than the conventional nine knots for a short period.

There were all sorts of snags surrounding the K-boats. It took a full five minutes to dive one of them; the long hulls made them difficult to handle; with an unpleasantly high accident rate, the average seaman was reluctant to serve in them; and, when they did come into service towards the end of the war, nobody could decide what to do with them. The concept in Jellicoe's mind was one of the casualties of the Battle of Jutland.

Another shortcoming of submarines was their armament. They had developed more quickly than their natural ally, the torpedo. As Lord Fisher put it, 'our torpedoes won't hit, and, when they do hit, produce no more effect than sawdust'. It was perfectly true. The range was no more than a thousand yards – which, in gunnery terms, was more or less point-blank. In 1915, a German torpedo had sunk a battleship built in 1901. Since the turn of the century, these vessels had become very much better protected. Ships such as HMS *Dreadnought* (completed in 1906) had practically nothing to fear from a submarine attack.

It might have been better to acknowledge their limitations and concentrate on smaller prey. The Admiralty, on the other hand, believed that if a submarine was to be accorded the status of warship she must be able to sink any other man-of-war. When, in 1916, the keel of *K18* was laid, the builders were suddenly informed of a change of plan. Instead of being used for the intended steam submarine, it would serve for a new type of vessel. Indeed, the keels of *K19*, *K20* and *K21* were to be employed for a similar purpose.

The newcomer that was to transform naval warfare was the *M1*. Unlike the K-boats, she was powered by conventional diesel-electric machinery. The area

A British 'K' class submarine, one of a steam-driven fleet.

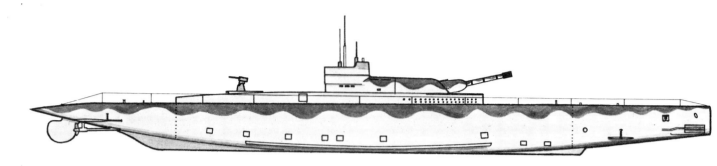

Britain's 'M' class submarines were nicknamed 'mutton boats'.

in front of her conning tower was occupied by a 12-inch gun (a battleship gun) weighing 60 tons. If everything worked satisfactorily, this would be loaded when the boat was submerged. She would then creep up on her target, surface, discharge the shell, and dive immediately afterwards. Ideally it should be possible to accomplish the operation in one minute. When they came into service, the *M1* and her two sisters (the *M4* was never completed) were known as 'submarine monitors'. The Royal Navy, with its knack of finding the right phrase, called them the 'mutton boats': seen in profile, the gun and its turret looked like a leg of mutton.

But there was a delay. Having conceived the M-boats, the Admiralty suddenly had misgivings. Suppose the secret were transmitted to Germany by a spy. Consider the effect on the Grand Fleet at Scapa Flow if a German 'mutton boat' suddenly appeared in its midst. The growing shape of the *M1* was draped in tarpaulins; the blueprints were hidden. No more work was done on the project for a year.

The *M1* and the *M2* were eventually completed in 1918; the *M3* followed in 1920. On 12 November 1925, the *M1* was lost with 69 officers and ratings 15 miles off Start Point in Devonshire. She had just dived when a Swedish cargo ship named the *Vidar* collided with her. The *Vidar*'s captain knew he had struck an underwater obstacle, but he had no idea it was a submarine. However, when the steamer was examined in dry dock at Kiel, traces of paint were found on her slightly damaged bow. Tests revealed they must have come from the *M1*. She was the fourth British submarine to be lost since the Armistice, in which time a total of 193 officers and men had perished.

By 1926 it had become obvious that the K-class boats would never amount to anything, and all but one of them were scrapped. The idea of the submarine working with the fleet was abandoned; the *M2* and the *M3* were assigned to experimental work. In 1927, the *M3* was converted into a minelayer and soldiered on until she was sold in 1932. The *M2* was less fortunate. During the war years, the *E22* had sallied forth into the North Sea with a seaplane mounted on her forecasing. The submarine had ferried the aircraft to a point near the enemy coast, from which it then took off and bombed nearby Zeppelin sheds. There was obviously much to be said for the idea of using a submarine as a minute aircraft carrier if it could be made to work.

A hangar with watertight doors thus replaced the gun in front of the *M2*'s conning tower; a launching catapult was added to her forecastle; and a small seaplane with folding wings named the *Peto* was assigned to her. On active service, it would clearly be impossible to bring the aircraft back on board, but that did not matter: it was deemed expendable.

On 26 January 1932, the *M2* was exercising in West Bay, not far from the Dorset coast. During the afternoon, a freighter bound from South Wales for Tyneside put in at Portland to bunker. In the course of conversation, the master asked a naval officer whether it was usual for submarines to dive stern first. No, he was told – they never did so. If he had seen such a thing, somebody was

obviously in trouble. The captain explained that he *had* seen such a thing – only an hour or so before, as he was approaching Portland Bill. After a search lasting eight days, the *M2* was discovered lying in 106 feet of water at the bottom of West Bay. Her hangar doors were open, and so was the hatch leading into the conning tower. The cause of the disaster was never completely discovered. According to one theory, the hangar doors were opened before she had properly surfaced; according to another, there was a defect in her hydroplanes. Whatever the reason, 60 officers and men had been killed.

While Britain was struggling to discover an attitude to submarines and their use in wartime, the other victorious powers of the First World War were seeking a formula for the comparative sizes of their navies. On 12 October 1921, the so-called First International Conference on Limitations of Naval Armaments was opened in Washington. Representatives of the United States, Great Britain, France, Italy and Japan attended. Britain was in the process of either scrapping or selling all her wartime submarines; nevertheless, with 137 boats, she now had the largest underwater fleet in the world. Among the terms of the Treaty of Versailles was a clause forbidding Germany to possess any U-boats. The assets of the conquered Imperial Navy were now reduced to a handful of very old surface ships. For that reason there seemed no point in inviting the Chancellor to send a delegate to Washington.

Despite her numerical superiority, Britain proposed that submarines should be abolished. The point was made yet again that they were no use except as commerce raiders – and then only if they broke the rules. The other powers opposed the suggestion. Apart from this, the treaty produced by the conference was effective. For example, it limited the size of battle fleets and severely restricted the size and rate of replacement of battleships. But its effect on submarine construction was negligible. Great Britain managed to coax an agreement from the other members that these vessels should not be used against merchant ships.

The *M2* was originally designed to carry a 12-inch gun. Later, she was adapted to transport the seaplane *Peto*. The experiment was a disastrous mistake and the *M2* was lost with all hands off the coast of Dorset.

69

But the phrasing was vague; it was uncertain whether they were totally forbidden this role, or whether they could attack commerce provided they stuck to the Cruiser Rules. In any case, France refused to ratify this part of the conclusions.

The delegates went back to their homes. In Great Britain, the energies of engineers and scientists were directed towards two projects. One was the very sensible proposition that, since the submarine was obviously going to remain a weapon of war, the best possible system of defence should be devised. The second was a return to the much trodden ground of developing a proper (as the Admiralty saw it) underwater warship.

During the past war, the only method of detecting the presence of an enemy submarine had been by hydrophones, which picked up the sound of it. This was all very well up to a point. But if the underwater craft switched off her engines and remained silent, there was no knowing she was there. Furthermore, all other vessels in the vicinity had to stop their own engines when hydrophones were used – otherwise their machinery would obscure the pattern of sound.

But now a better method was in the course of development. Known as asdic (after the Allied Submarine Detection Investigation Committee that had been set up in 1917), it was the brainchild of an American named Herbert Grove Dorsey. The principle was that sound could be bounced off a metal hull, producing an echo at distances of up to a mile or so, which could also supply such essential information as the range and bearing of the submarine.

RIGHT Upon completion, the *X1* was the largest submarine in the world.

BELOW The British submarine *X1*, seen here at Malta, was conceived as a submersible cruiser. She was immense, armed with 5·2-inch guns, but unfortunately, her engines were a constant source of trouble.

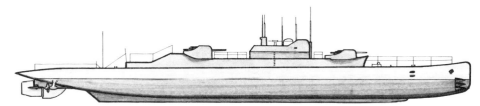

The project to build a submarine as a complete man-of-war was awe-inspiring. The vessel that eventually came into service in 1925 was a kind of underwater cruiser. Known as the *X1*, she displaced over 3000 tons. Four 5·2-inch guns were mounted on her hull in double turrets; her two diesel engines gave her a surface speed of 18·5 knots, and she could travel halfway round the world without refuelling.

Unfortunately, the engines of *X1* turned out to be unreliable. The unhappy boat (was the Royal Navy's determination to keep on calling submarines 'boats' an indication of contempt?) spent most of her time in dockyards until, in 1937, she was scrapped.

But the idea of giant submarines was catching on. The French matched the *X1* with the *Surcouf* – which carried a seaplane, two 8-inch guns, and 22 torpedoes. The Americans built the *Argonaut*, a vessel of 2710 tons and the first of many able to cope with the large distances of the Pacific. But the last word on immense submarines came from the Japanese who produced three vessels – each of them 400 feet long and with a surface displacement of 3530 tons. They carried three aircraft, the components of a fourth, and a launching catapult. The *Surcouf* and the *Argonaut* both survived to take part in the Second World War. The former went missing on 18 April 1942. The latter was rammed by Japanese destroyers in the Bismarck Sea later that year.

In its day, the First World War was described as 'the war to end all wars'. It was a delightful idea; but a decade afterwards a mood of disillusion had already set in. It appeared unlikely that human aggression had at last been contained, and that the clash of arms would no more resound. The question, of course, was who would fight whom? Germany was disarmed and virtually bankrupt. Trouble, surely, could not be expected from that quarter. France, whose submarine contribution to the events of 1914–18 had been small, seemed to be showing an unhealthy interest in these vessels. Japan was inscrutable as became an oriental power, and was certainly not showing the doglike devotion of a former ally. America's interest had become focused on large submersibles that could take the Pacific in their stride. Great Britain glanced uneasily at her China Station, and decided to reinforce its underwater strike power. The result of this decision was the O, the P and the R classes. The first of them, HMS *Oberon*, was completed in 1926.

Oberon, in many ways, anticipated the shape of submarines to come. She was the first to be equipped with asdic, and the first to be fitted with a 40-foot periscope. The latter feature meant that she could maintain periscope depth and yet remain safe from any attempt to ram her. To increase her range, she was provided with extra tanks, built on the upper section outside her pressure hull. These were the shortcomings of the O class – just as they were of the P-boats and the R-boats. No matter how hard the engineers tried, they could not prevent them from leaking. Wherever *Oberon* and the others went, their presence was made plain by tell-tale slicks of oil that streamed in the vessels' wakes.

The Washington Treaty was due to expire in 1936. In 1930, the representatives of America, Great Britain, France, Italy and Japan again assembled round a table – this time in London. As before, Germany was not invited. By now, the British submarine fleet had become the second smallest of the five powers. Indeed, numerically the biggest belonged to Russia with a total of 150. But these were split up between four fleets – the Arctic, the Baltic, the Black Sea, and the Far East. Furthermore, the majority of them were small coastal submarines, and not to be taken seriously.

When the United Kingdom delegate again put forward a plea for the abolition of submarines, Italy was the only power to agree. But, the delegate from Rome insisted, this must depend on the scrapping of battle fleets as well. The others laughed politely, and went on to the next piece of business. Eventually, it was decided that a limit of 2000 tons and 5·1-inch guns should be imposed on new

With the 'O' class submarines, built for service in the Far East, the British designers returned to more orthodox ideas. The *Oxley* was built by Vickers Armstrong at Barrow in 1926 and was lost on active service, 10 September 1939

submarines. For good measure, the United States and Japan pledged themselves to confine the size of their underwater fleets to that of Britain's, i.e. a total of 52,700 tons. France, which made no such concession, now had the world's largest effective force with 82,000 tons.

The fact that Germany had been banned by the Treaty of Versailles from owning submarines did not mean that the nation was not interested in the subject any longer. Nor did it mean that it was not developing its expertise. Indeed, it had already constructed the prototypes for two members of a new generation of U-boats. The mastermind of these clandestine activities was the great armourer of Germany, the black baron of the Ruhr, Gustav von Krupp.

During the war, a company in The Hague named Blessing and Co. had been importing an uncommon amount of iron ore. It was much more than enough to meet the total requirements of Holland, which was not surprising. After its arrival at a Dutch port, the ore was quietly transported to Essen in Germany. One hundred per cent of Blessing and Co.'s shares were owned by Krupp.

Some while later, Blessing's sold itself to the firm of Hollandsche Industrie en Handel Maatschappij. The name was changed to Siderius AG Siderius, and it became the holding company for three shipyards. The capital was owned by two Krupp directors; in 1922, 40 German engineers were appointed to the staff. To give it a veneer of respectability, Krupp now began to unload blocks of shares on to influential Dutch citizens. In 1926, another office was set up in The Hague under the name of Ingenieur-Kantoor voor Scheepsbouw. Two lieutenant-commanders from the German navy and 30 workers from the Germaniawerft at Kiel moved in, and a U-boat construction office was set up.

The new venture began by sending submarine blueprints to Japan. Presently, it was selling them to Spain, Finland, Turkey – and to Holland itself. From designing submarines, it was not a very great step to building them. Sure enough, orders were received from Spain, Finland and Turkey. Gustav Krupp insisted that the Ingenieur-Kantoor voor Scheepsbouw 'must have no traceable connection with the Germaniawerft'. The Spanish boat was, indeed, built at Cadiz. It displaced 740 tons and, later, served as a prototype for the *U25* and *U26*. The Finnish deal produced the specifications for the *Us 1–24*; the Turkish vessel, which should have been named *Batiray*, was never delivered.

All these ventures were closely observed by members of the Germaniawerft. Apprentices were brought from Kiel to watch the various processes of construction. When the boats were completed, they were subjected to unusually exhaustive trials. The crews employed were German; quite apart from testing the ideas and the workmanship, they provided excellent opportunities to gain experience in U-boat handling.

In 1933 Adolf Hitler came to power. One of his first acts was to repudiate the Versailles Treaty. Krupp was ready; he was already building sheds at Kiel for the construction of U-boats. At the same time, Karl Doenitz, the wartime

ABOVE Despite the ban on U-boats resulting from the Treaty of Versailles, the German house of Krupp continued to work on them. A 740-ton boat, built at Cadiz for the Spanish government, served as a prototype for the *U25* (shown here) and the *U26*.

BELOW By 1933 Krupp's Germaniawerft at Kiel was equipped to build submarines again. In that year, six vessels were ordered from the shipyard.

Examining torpedoes aboard a U-boat.

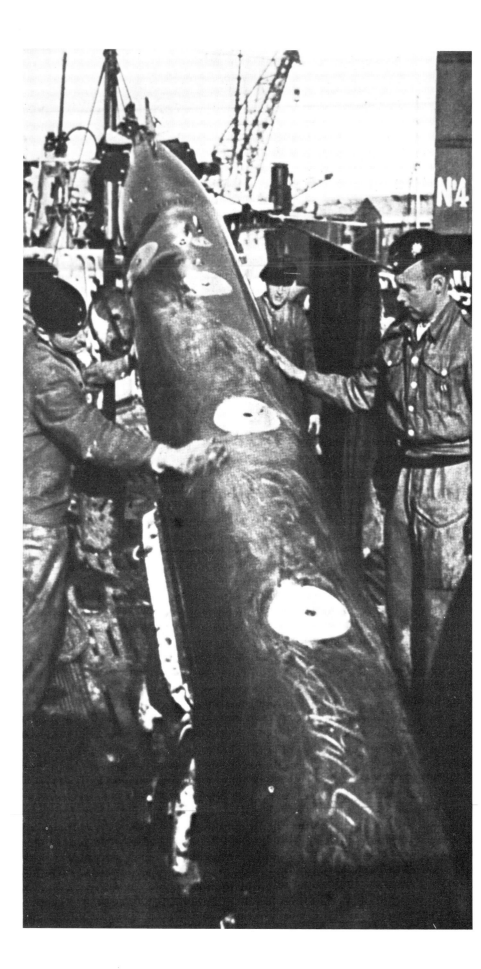

U-boat commander who had spent those reflective months in a British prisoner-of-war camp, was working on a new concept of submarine tactics. Known as the 'wolf-pack', the idea was to match a concentration of convoy escort vessels by a comparable concentration of submarines.

On 18 June 1935 Hitler remarked to the C-in-C of his navy, Admiral Erich Raeder, 'Today is the happiest day of my life.' The reason for the Führer's jubilation was that an Anglo-German naval agreement had just been signed in London. Under the terms, Germany agreed to restrict her sea-power to thirty-five per cent of the United Kingdom's. There was, however, an exception. Her submarine strength could be forty-five per cent of the UK's – and in exceptional circumstances, and provided she gave adequate notice, it could be one hundred per cent.

In view of the mauling that Great Britain had received from U-boats a mere 18 years before, such terms may seem surprising. However, as the British government was obviously aware, Hitler had been building submarines since 1933, when he ordered six such vessels from Germaniawerft and insisted that they should prepare to launch one a month until further notice. It was, perhaps, best to rationalize the situation. What was more, at least half the fleet destroyers were now equipped with asdic, and it was planned to include it in all future vessels of this type. With the method of detecting hostile boats assured, and a strike power of 30 depth charges per escort available, the day of the submarine was indeed over. That, at any rate, was what they thought in Whitehall.

The years of experiment were now largely ended. Britain and America were concentrating on the minimum number of types, each designed for a particular theatre of operations (in the UK the S-boats were intended for operations in the North Sea, and the T-boats to replace the O, P and R-boats). Germany was doing what she had done before – concentrating on simplicity and mass production. Presumably acting on the assumption that, having lost one war, she must go back to the start and shake a six, she began the numbering all over again with *U1*. In times to come, any researcher who has nothing better to do might occupy his mind with the question of why, when everybody else was now giving their submarines names, Germany continued to stick to the more functional *U1*, *U2*, etc. designations. Was it that a number generates less sentiment than a name; and that therefore the captains might be more ready to hazard themselves and their vessels in the course of duty?

But two fields of experiment remained active. A Dutch naval officer named Commander I. I. Wichers had already invented the *schnorkel* – a breathing tube that enabled boats to run their diesel engines and recharge their batteries when submerged (it was incorporated into U-boats in 1943). It was an important step forward, but it was not sufficient to produce the perfect submarine: such a vessel would be able to travel at high speeds when submerged – without *ever* needing to surface. A German engineer and scientist named Professor Hellmuth Walther began work on the problem in 1937. By the outbreak of the Second World War, it looked as if he were already close to a solution. It involved an entirely new system for submerged propulsion, using Ingolin (a highly concentrated form of hydrogen peroxide) as fuel. Calculations suggested that it provided 35 times the amount of energy that could be stored in an electric battery – giving a speed underwater of 25 knots for at least three hours, and an acceptable – if slower – speed for very much longer.

In the same year that Professor Walther began his experiments, Commodore Karl Doenitz – now flag officer in charge of Germany's U-boat arm – carried out the first manoeuvres using 'wolf-pack' tactics. They were held in the Baltic; by all accounts, they were extremely encouraging.

6 Wolf-pack

You cannot write a reasonable peace treaty unless you have a proper understanding of a war's causes. Had the Allied statesmen been better aware of the reasons for the 1914–18 holocaust, the terms of Versailles might have been more generous. This, in its turn, might have prevented the Second World War. But the conditions were harsh; the years of peace no more than an interlude. Just over two decades after the armistice, the U-boats were returning to the North Atlantic hunting grounds. They were, in some respects, improved U-boats; in essentials, however, they were not unlike the vessels in which their crews' fathers had sailed.

Ever since he had been put in charge of Germany's submarine arm back in 1935, Karl Doenitz had been developing his philosophy. It should have come as no surprise to Britain. The salient points appeared in Doenitz's book, *Die U-bootwaffe*, published by the Berlin firm of E. S. Mittler in 1939. Anyone could buy a copy, and presumably it found its way into the British Admiralty. But the notion that asdic and depth charges had sounded the knell of submarine warfare died hard. A recurrence of the events of the First World War, which had brought Britain so close to disaster, was unthinkable. That, perhaps, was the difference; Doenitz had profited by the lessons of history – the thinking sailors of Whitehall chose to ignore them.

The British Admiralty was not prepared for Doenitz; nor, it might be said, was the German. The Kommodore's ideas (he was promoted to Rear-Admiral in October 1939) were based on what he called 'wolf-pack' tactics. One boat would sight the convoy. It would fall back and signal the position to others. While it maintained contact from a distance, the rest of the strike force would converge on the prey. Operating mostly on the surface, they would swarm in among the columns of merchantmen, causing fearful destruction. Not the least of their advantages was the fact that, using their diesel engines, they could outpace the slower escort vessels. Indeed, with the aid of supply ships, they could execute their attacks in areas beyond the range of aircraft and destroyers.

Despite the fact that, on manoeuvres in the Baltic, wolf-pack tactics had already shown their value, the C-in-C of the German Navy, Grand Admiral Erich Raeder, refused to be impressed. Doenitz on the other hand insisted that, given 300 submarines on station in the Atlantic, Britain could be starved to death. To achieve this, 1000 U-boats would be required. Each should be a vessel of about 500 tons: able to dive quickly, be extremely manoeuvrable, and armed with four torpedo tubes in the bows and one at the stern.

RIGHT The schnorkel, a device that enabled a submarine to run its diesel engines when submerged, was invented by a Dutch naval officer in the late 1930s. Behind it, in this picture, is the boat's search periscope.

OPPOSITE Admiral Speer and Commodore Doenitz reviewing U-boats after exercises in the Baltic. The occasion was the trying of Doenitz's wolf-pack tactics. As he had predicted, they were extremely successful.

Doenitz's hunters

ABOVE Photographs taken by one of the crew aboard this U-boat.

But Raeder was a battleship man. He believed that submarines should be large, cruiser-type vessels – operating independently. Doenitz's argument made little impact on him. In any case, he had other worries. The Grand Admiral had not expected war with Britain and France, and the declaration on 3 September 1939 found him unprepared. Above all things, he was anxious about his country's lack of large surface warships. 'If they had to grapple with the British fleet', he wrote, 'they would be just about able to die with dignity.' All his energies were devoted to implementing the so-called Z-Plan that had been devised at the end of 1938. The programme of shipbuilding contained in it stipulated 25 battleships and battle cruisers, 8 aircraft carriers, but only 162 submarines capable of operating in the Atlantic. Nor, at first, did there seem to be any urgency about it. In January 1939, Hitler had assured Raeder that, 'For my political aims, I shall not need the Fleet before 1946.' On 3 September 1939, when Britain and France declared war against Germany, the Führer's reaction to Raeder was, simply, 'What now?'

At the time, Doenitz's U-boat fleet amounted to 56 vessels – 46 of which were ready for action. But, of this total, only 22 were suitable for operations in the Atlantic. The remainder were small submarines that could not stray beyond the North Sea. The first sinking did, indeed, occur on the very day that war broke out – though whether it was of any value to Germany is doubtful.

The *U30*, commanded by twenty-five-year-old Lieut. Fritz-Julius Lemp, was on station south of Rockall in the Atlantic. Looming up ahead, Lemp saw the 13,581-ton Anchor liner *Athenia* on passage from Britain to the United States. According to the U-boat captain, the *Athenia* was steering a zig-zag course away from the normal shipping routes. He assumed that she was a troopship. Having made certain that she was British, he fired two torpedoes at her. They homed faultlessly on the target, and the *Athenia* sank. As it happened, all but 112 of the 1400 people aboard her were rescued. But that was not the point. On the very first day of war, Lieut. Lemp had defied international law, which was still based on the Cruiser Rules. When Hitler heard about it, he was furious. Doenitz immediately signalled his U-boat captains: 'By order of the Führer passenger ships until further notice will not be attacked, even if in convoy.' The pages recording the action were removed from the *U30*'s log, and a somewhat chastened Lieut. Lemp was urged to be more careful in future.

Perhaps the *Athenia* was particularly unfortunate. At the time, there was a very reasonable chance that the two torpedoes might not have exploded. A salvo fired at the aircraft carrier HMS *Ark Royal* did no more than dent her plates; and there were other, similar, incidents. The fault lay in the firing mechanism. It was not, however, sufficiently prevalent to save the lives of the aircraft carrier HMS *Courageous* and 518 of her complement. Escorted by destroyers, the carrier was steaming through the western approaches to the English Channel on 17 September, when she crossed the path of the *U29*. The boat's commanding officer, Lieut-Cdr Schuhardt, had her under observation for two hours before she came into range. Then, at precisely the right moment, the *Courageous* happened to change direction – presenting her ample side to the lurking submarine. Schuhardt ordered three torpedoes to be fired. Without waiting to watch the result, he crash dived. At 250 feet, he heard the explosions of four depth charges, but the *U29* managed to wriggle away to safety. Unlike the affair of the *Athenia*, there was nothing shameful about sending an aircraft carrier to the bottom.

Gunther Prien of the *U47* did even better. Throughout the First World War, it had been the constant ambition of U-boat commanders to penetrate the British fleet's anchorage at Scapa Flow. None of the attempts succeeded. Doenitz, however, believed that it was possible, and Prien was given the assignment. The date was 13 October. The operation was carefully planned – though in one particular, conditions turned against it. The night had been chosen on the assumption that there would be no moonlight. There was not; but, as if to make good his deficiency, a magnificent display of aurora borealis lit up the sky. Nevertheless, Prien decided to go ahead, which was just as well. If he had postponed the attack by a day or so, he would have found the channel blocked. As things were, the precaution had not yet been carried out.

As an example of courage, brilliant seamanship and cool thinking there is little to equal the feat of Prien and his crew. From the assortment of potential victims, he selected the battleship HMS *Royal Oak*. Of the four torpedoes discharged from his bow tubes, one misfired – and only one of the remaining three hit the target. The damage caused by it was negligible. At this point, prudence might have suggested to Prien that he should call the operation off and head for safety. But strangely enough the solitary hit did not seem to have attracted any attention. He waited until the tubes had been reloaded. Then he fired a second salvo. This time, they crashed home with devastating effect. The *Royal Oak* erupted – within 13 minutes, she had turned over on to her side and was sinking. Twenty-four officers and 809 men went with her. The *U47* turned away from the scene of her triumph and went home to Germany.

ABOVE U-boat rescue operations were as fraught with peril as their attacks.

RIGHT The *U47*, which sank HMS *Royal Oak*

But, although Doenitz seemed to be the only senior German naval officer with faith in the idea, the business of U-boats lay out in the ocean. The sinking of such giants as the *Courageous* and the *Royal Oak* were undoubtedly spectacular, but the natural prey of these vessels was that unglamorous drudge of commerce, the merchant ship. In 1917, Germany had nearly brought Britain to her knees by putting a stranglehold on her trade with America. This, surely, should be the way of things in the Second World War. But Raeder preferred to invest

Anti-submarine war: the depth charge
crew of a Royal Navy patrol service
trawler in the North Sea, March 1942.

his faith in battleships; and Hitler, who had a very imperfect understanding of the sea (he was, after all, a native of land-locked Austria), agreed with him.[4] Although the destruction of the *Royal Oak* had brought the U-boat supremo into favour, he was still a long way short of his thousand-strong fleet.

Nevertheless, Atlantic practice was already showing that the wolf-pack tactics were as effective as the Baltic exercises had suggested. On land, too, events were running in favour of Doenitz. With the overthrow of France in the summer of 1940, it became possible to establish U-boat bases as far south as Bordeaux – and at Brest, which overlooked the very approaches to the Channel. It was now no longer necessary to make the arduous journey to the Atlantic from German ports via the north of Scotland. A U-boat commander could devote less time to travelling and more to his deadly purpose.

The ethics of the profession were still a matter for discussion. The Cruiser Rules had been written for surface ships – and, while it was possible to apply them to a raider such as the *Graf Spee*, they were obviously beyond the capability of submarines. A British captain once found himself in a perfect position to sink

BELOW The control room of a British submarine during an attack. The captain (centre) is at the periscope; the ladder in the foreground leads to the conning tower.

the German liner *Bremen*; but, if she were alone, he would have to hold his fire. So far as he could tell there seemed to be a Luftwaffe aircraft in the vicinity. Did this count as an escort? He surfaced to investigate; the aeroplane spotted him, and he was forced to crash dive. By the time he was ready for action, the *Bremen* was several miles away.

HMS *Thunderbolt* was originally named HMS *Thetis*. As the *Thetis*, she was lost on her shipyard trials in 1939, killing all but three of the men on board. She was salvaged, and renamed. She was destroyed in the Mediterranean on 13 March 1943.

Hitler had begun the war by urging strict compliance with international law. Gradually, however, his chivalrous zeal evaporated. On 17 July 1940, he declared a total blockade of the United Kingdom, and gave his U-boat captains the right to attack even neutral shipping on sight.

By this time, a high proportion of the British warships that might have been escorting shipping were patrolling the English Channel against the possibility of an invasion. On 2 September, Britain signed an agreement with the United States in which 50 ancient USN destroyers were transferred to the Royal Navy in return for the leases of certain bases in the Western Hemisphere. For the moment, however, the U-boats were having things their own way. The pickings were so good and the hazards so small that their crews referred to this period as the 'happy time'. In June 1940, 58 ships adding up to 284,000 tons were sunk on their way across the Atlantic. The figures rose steadily until, in October, 63 vessels totalling 352,000 tons were destroyed. Lieut-Cdr Schultze of the *U48* became the first captain to account for 100,000 tons of shipping. Before long, he was overtaken by the intrepid Prien, who was heading for the 200,000 mark. All this was accomplished at the cost of six U-boats.

If the word 'submarine' means a vessel that belongs naturally to the world beneath the surface, a carrion craft that spends all its life under the sea, then the true submarine had not yet been built. The U-boats of this period might better be described as submersibles. Doenitz himself came very close to the truth, when he referred to them as 'diving vessels'. They could, to be sure, travel far beneath the waves; but only for limited periods and at considerably reduced speeds. They were at their most effective on top of the water, matching and even exceeding the speeds of the escort vessels. They out-ranged them from their French bases; and, when they were not submerged, asdic could do nothing to detect them.

Even after they had dived, asdic had its limitations. It could indicate the presence of a U-boat; it could even divulge such important matters as its bearing and range. But the depth charges were released over the stern. During this moment of truth, a blind spot occurred. The target, which had once been pin-pointed, vanished. All that remained was human judgement.

In early 1941, the losses to merchantmen were greater than the rate of replacement. On 6 March, Winston Churchill issued his famous 'Battle of the Atlantic' directive, in which he gave priority to the destruction of U-boats. Later that month, an improvement in the escorting of convoys began to bite. On 17 March, the destroyer *Wolverine* sank the *U47*. There were no survivors. Gunther Prien, the hero of Scapa Flow, was dead. Ten days later, the *U99* and the *U100* were disposed of by destroyers guarding a convoy. Otto Kretschmer, commander of the former, was taken prisoner; Joachim Schepke, captain of the *U100*, died with the rest of the crew. Both were star performers; the U-boat pack was now stripped of its aces. And when *U551* was sunk by a trawler, it was estimated that one-fifth of Doenitz's Atlantic fleet had been destroyed. The happy time was over – at any rate, for the time being.

Indeed, when the battleship *Bismarck* went down, the *U74* inadvertently contributed to the loss of life. She arrived on the scene when the cruiser

ABOVE The crew of HMS *Storm* with a symbol of the submarine's achievements. The bars on the flag indicate sinkings by torpedo; the stars, vessels destroyed by her guns; each dot marks the end of a schooner; and the dagger denotes a secret mission.

OPPOSITE June 1941: 21-in torpedoes on the deck of the old cruiser HMS *Forth*, serving as a sub-depotship to the submarine lying alongside her at Holy Loch, Scotland.

Dorsetshire and the destroyer *Maori* were picking up survivors. Foolishly, perhaps, the U-boat's captain raised his periscope. It was seen by the British men-of-war, which promptly abandoned the rescue operation. As it happened, the *U74* had used up all her torpedoes, but who was to know? She picked up three of the *Bismarck*'s men and then she, too, departed. The remainder were left to drown.

Three months later, an unhappy freak of chance brought the *U570* to the surface directly beneath a Hudson bomber of the RAF's Coastal Command. The aircraft went into the attack; the U-boat's captain surrendered. Eventually warships towed the captured submarine to Northern Ireland – where, under the name of HMS *Graph*, she joined the Royal Navy.

But, despite these losses, the U-boat fleet was growing. By 1 September 1941, it was estimated that 200 had been commissioned – 47 had been sunk since the outbreak of war. Doenitz was now planning to send his larger vessels farther afield – for example, to the waters off the Cape of Good Hope, where the traffic was heavy and the opportunities rich. But in the autumn Hitler had fresh instructions for Doenitz. A sizeable force of U-boats must be diverted to the Mediterranean to shore up the flagging efforts of the Italians. On 25 November, one of them (*U331*) penetrated a screen of destroyers and sank the battleship *Barham* with the loss of 859 lives. The aircraft carrier *Ark Royal* was sunk at last, and so was the cruiser *Galatea*. In the Atlantic, however, the rate of merchant ship losses moderated – in October, only 32 (157,000 tons) were destroyed. If this was disappointing to the staff of U-Boat Command in their offices at the Steinplatz, Berlin, they had only the Führer to blame. German aircraft were reaping a sufficiently rich harvest in the Mediterranean without the need to send submarines from the Atlantic.[5]

More significant, however, was the fate of convoy number HG76 and the submarines that lay in wait for it. HG76 was due to sail from Gibraltar for Britain in early December 1941. At the last moment, however, its departure was postponed until the escort had been increased to 13 ships. Among them was the former German liner *Hannover*. Early in the war, the *Hannover* had been seized as a prize. By the simple expedient of replacing her superstructure by a flight deck, she had been converted into an escort carrier. Her name was changed to HMS *Audacity*.

Predictably, the wolf-packs came out in force against HG76 as its ships struggled northwards through the turbulent waters of the Bay of Biscay. As one attack was beaten off, reinforcements arrived to thrust home another. One of the casualties was HMS *Audacity*; but, when the journey was over, only two merchantmen had been lost. It was a small price to pay for the destruction of five U-boats.

On 7 December 1941, the Japanese attacked Pearl Harbor, and the United

The German *XXI* travelled at 17 knots submerged, just beyond the 15-mile range of Allied sonar and asdic equipment; however, boats of this type were never used in combat.

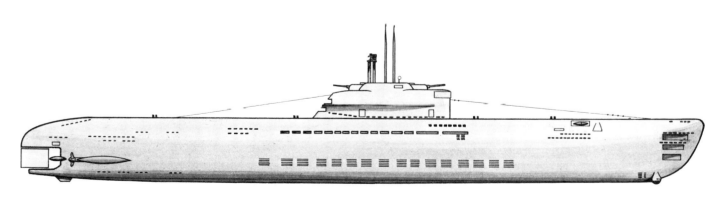

The *U570* was taken by the Royal Navy after an attack by a Hudson bomber. She was brought back to the UK and renamed HMS *Graph*.

States came into the war. Ever since 1940 a US naval mission had been established in London. The Royal Navy had passed on information to its members about convoy experiences and on the development of anti-submarine techniques. The main lesson at this time was to use convoys at all costs – even if the escort forces had to be weak.

Whatever was learned in London does not appear to have crossed the Atlantic. Within days of the United States's declaration of war, Doenitz launched operation *Paukenschlag* ('roll on the drums'). Aware that the bulk of the United States Navy was involved against the Japanese in the Pacific, he expected reasonable results from an offensive against merchant shipping off the eastern seaboard of North America. In fact, the sinkings were on such a scale that they surprised him. The Americans had paid little attention to those discussions in London. Hardly any of the merchantmen were in convoy; and those that were had only token escorts. Their captains were making free use of their radios – at night they sailed with all their lights blazing. It was too easy. Even at its peak, it seems unlikely that more than a dozen U-boats were employed in the operation. Between them, by the end of January, they had sunk the better part of 327,000 tons of shipping. Their kills ranged from the coast of Newfoundland down to the Caribbean, where the harvest of tankers was especially rich.

RIGHT Doenitz argued long and hard to convince the German Navy that U-boats could be its most important weapon. German officers examine submarine models – but Doenitz's operational fleet in 1939 numbered only forty-six.

CENTRE Scouting the Atlantic.

FAR RIGHT Back in the North Atlantic, U-boats enjoyed unprecedented success: 352,000 tons of Allied shipping were destroyed between June and October 1940.

BELOW Submarines alongside HMS *Forth*, June 1943. On the right is the former German *U570* which became HMS *Graph*

OPPOSITE BELOW M. Bone's impression of HM *Tradwind* under construction prior to the Second World War.

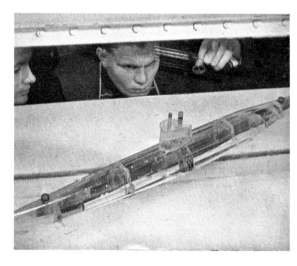

This was the beginning of what the U-boat crews fondly called the second 'happy time'. When, in May, the USN at last introduced convoys, Doenitz switched the concentration of his wolf-packs back into mid-Atlantic. The year that had begun so well showed no signs of deteriorating. During the first six months of 1942, 585 merchant ships (three million tons) were sunk. Of 100 new U-boats commissioned, 21 were lost – and, of those, only 6 were destroyed in the Western Atlantic. There were now U-boats operating as far away as the South Atlantic and even into the Indian Ocean. At one time, they were linking up with Japanese boats at Penang.

On these long voyages, the problem of refuelling was overcome by the introduction of tanker submarines – or, as they were more commonly called, 'milch cows'. These were large submarines of 1600 tons that were not manoeuvrable enough for operations against shipping. They were stripped of all their armament except deck guns for protection. Fully laden, they could carry 700 tons of fuel – of which 600 were available to their clientele of smaller U-boats. One of their trading posts was a patch of ocean in the region of the Azores.

In July 1942, the American and British governments rationalized the system of escorts by dividing the Atlantic into two. West of longitude 47°W, it became the responsibility of the US Navy Department in Washington; east of it, the British Admiralty took over. The division was known as 'the Chop Line'.

So far, events were going well for Doenitz and his U-boat commanders. On 25 January 1943, a meeting took place at the Führer's headquarters in Germany that promised even better things. At last Hitler was compelled to admit that there was no future for Germany in maintaining a large surface fleet. The battleships and the cruisers were to be phased out, and the nation's entire dockyard capacity devoted to the construction and repairs of U-boats. Two weeks later. Raeder resigned as C-in C. His place was taken by Doenitz.

Had they been aware of it, however, Doenitz and his colleagues would have had small cause for celebrations. In 1940, Hitler had made the disastrous mistake of dismissing radar as unimportant, and calling a stop to all research for a period of one year. The Allies had introduced 1·5-metre sets which were used for spotting submarines on the surface. They were countered by Metox – a device popularly known as the 'Biscay Cross' (after its clumsy aerial fashioned in the shape of a cross). It could pick up enemy transmissions and even sound automatic warnings to U-boat crews. But, by this time, Allied scientists were working on a more sophisticated system – the short wave, centimetric version. It enabled escort vessels and aircraft to locate a surfaced U-boat at a range of several miles. What was more, the Biscay Cross was unable to detect it.

At about this time the technicians developed heavier depth charges and a device known as the 'hedgehog'. Instead of dropping them astern, it threw them in clusters ahead of the escort – and thereby eliminated asdic's blind spot. And, in September 1942, the first of the 'Support Groups' had been planned. Made up of highly trained warships (and usually including a carrier), they were to be used as mobile reserves that could be rushed to reinforce a threatened convoy. Fortunately for the peace of mind of U-boat crews, the heavy demands of trooping caused their introduction to be delayed for six months.

On 12 September 1942, the *U156* sank the homeward-bound British troopship *Laconia* at a point some distance south of the equator. The *U156* had just completed a rendezvous with a milch cow, and several other U-boats were replenishing their supplies of fuel from the vessel.

As it happened, the *Laconia* had been carrying 1800 Italian prisoners-of-war. Once the *U156*'s captain, Lieut-Cdr Hartenstein, realized this he sent out a message *en clair*, asking for assistance with the rescue work. Any Allied vessel that took part was promised immunity from attack. Some of the other U-boats also joined in.

No doubt the signal was picked up in Whitehall – just as it was received in Berlin. It does not, however, appear to have reached Ascension Island. The *U156* was now crammed with survivors, and she had three lifeboats in tow. The idea was to meet up with a French warship that had been dispatched from Dakar. At some point in mid-ocean, the passengers would be transferred.

Hartenstein was about to get under way when a speck appeared in the sky. It was an American Liberator bomber from the US base on Ascension Island. The aircraft circled the scene, lost height and released its bombs. In what seemed to be a matter of seconds, Hartenstein transferred the *Laconia* survivors from the submarine to the already overcrowded lifeboats. He cut them adrift and crash dived. By some miracle, the U-boat escaped unscathed – and so did the *U506*, which was attacked by a seaplane when she had 102 unexpected guests from the liner on board. As a result of this unfortunate episode, Doenitz ordered: 'All attempts to rescue the crews of sunken ships will cease forthwith.' The last strands of compassion had been cut. The final vestige of the chivalrous Cruiser Rules had been demolished by a couple of ill-advised (or misinformed) airmen.

At the end of 1942, the wolf-packs were out in force in the Atlantic. So far as their crews could see, the second 'happy time' was far from over. In the four months of July to October, they had sunk 396 ships (two million tons). During the same period, 61 new boats had been commissioned, bringing the total to 365. On the debit side, 32 U-boats had been lost.

Two U-boats operating together somewhere in the North Atlantic.

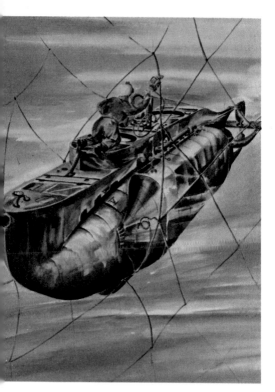

The British 'X' class was a group of midget submarines specifically designed to destroy the German battleship, *Tirpitz*. A watercolour (1945) by J. Brook depicts a diver using a pneumatic cutter to sever the net which is the obstacle to the *X-24*'s mission.

What was more, conditions had changed since 1939. The Allied navies now had the power of detection, the power of destruction, and the power of air cover. Many convoys now had their own aircraft carriers – vessels of about 8000 tons that had been laid down as bulk transports. True to their original purpose, they were loaded with oil or grain, but each was fitted with a flight deck able to accommodate four fighters.

Even though a bomber equipped with centimetric radar had been shot down near Rotterdam, and the Germans had been able to examine its instruments, they refused to believe in it. The more senior officers preferred to take the word of a captured RAF pilot, who professed that Allied aviators beamed on the Biscay Crosses. At lower levels, there was talk of a secret weapon. It was, indeed, a terrifying experience to be lying on the surface beneath a comforting canopy of cloud – and then to watch an aircraft dive from the murk, bang on target, creating a sudden havoc of destruction. Nowhere, it seemed, could be considered safe, and even the provision of flak guns gave small protection. Eventually, Doenitz ordered his captains, 'On confirming detection by aircraft, U-boats to dive forthwith and remain submerged for forty minutes.' It was, perhaps, an admission of defeat.

But defeat was certainly not apparent in March 1943. Two convoys were outward bound across the Atlantic from New York – the HX229 and the slower SC122. All told, 100 ships had originally been involved. In the early stages of the voyage, however, westerly gales had scattered the merchantmen, and 20 had turned back. There were now 80 of them concentrated in a relatively small area. Unknown to their captains, 44 U-boats – members of the *Dränger*, the *Raubgraf*, and the *Stürmer* groups – were lurking in the vicinity. The wolves were there, and so were the sheep – but there were no signs of the shepherds. So far as the U-boat commanders could see, the HX229 was escorted only by two destroyers and a pair of corvettes.

For five days, the U-boats launched an almost continuous series of attacks. Despite reinforcements that were hurried on to the scene, the Allies lost 21 ships adding up to 141,000 tons. As Churchill wrote to President Roosevelt afterwards, 'Our escorts are everywhere too thin, and the strain upon the British Navy is becoming intolerable.' When, at last, the attacks came to an end on 20 March, it was because the U-boat crews were exhausted. It was, as U-boat Command proudly announced, 'the biggest success to date'.

The British Admiralty was worried; but so, strangely enough, were the architects of submarine warfare in the Steinplatz at Berlin. Most of the sinkings had taken place on the first night. After that, the opposition had increased to 'menacing proportions'. Few people at U-boat Command believed that the best was yet to come. The best had already occurred.

Winter abdicated in favour of early spring; the U-boat attacks continued; and more Allied merchantmen were painfully put to death. But then, in early May, the tide changed. The anti-submarine support groups were now ready for action. The measure of their effectiveness became apparent during the first week of May, when the convoy ONS5 sailed from Britain for America. Again, the prelude was a spell of gale force winds. When the ships reached a point off the southeasterly tip of Greenland, 44 U-boats (belonging to the *Amsel*, *Drossel*, *Fink*, and *Star* groups) were barring the passage. There were now more submarines than there were merchant ships. The odds might have seemed to favour a carnage on the lines of that suffered by convoy HX229.

But now there was no lack of warships, nor of air power, nor of fast reserves. When the last torpedo had been fired, the convoy had lost 12 of its 42 ships. U-boat casualties amounted to 7. The escort groups had seen action at last. What was more, they worked.

When Doenitz heard about it, he commented that the U-boats 'are unquestionably outmatched and in a hopeless position'. Later, to his captains, he

signalled, 'The enemy in his efforts to deprive the U-boat of its invisibility has developed a system of radio-location which puts him several lengths ahead of us. I am fully aware of all the difficulties you encounter in fighting the convoy defence forces. Rest assured that as your Commander-in-Chief I have done, and will continue to do, everything to change the situation as soon as possible ...'

On 24 May, he recalled all the U-boat groups from the North Atlantic. Nevertheless, he still maintained that 'On success or failure in the Battle of the Atlantic depends the whole outcome of the war.' If this were the yardstick, the war was already lost.

The U-boat menace was over. Sinkings became confined to what Doenitz called 'soft spots' – remote areas in which they could strike with impunity. The introduction of the schnorkel in 1943 enabled the vessels to charge their batteries without coming to the surface. But the real breakthrough in submarine technology arrived too late. At the start of the war, Professor Hellmuth Walther had been working on a vessel powered by concentrated hydrogen peroxide. It would, he had promised, be able to travel at 25 knots submerged. Known as the type XXVI, and armed with 10 torpedo tubes, 100 were ordered in the spring of 1944. By the time the war ended, only 4 had been completed – and these were still in the trial stages.

On 4 May 1945, all U-boats were ordered to cease operations. One hundred and fifty-six surrendered themselves – the remaining 221 were scuttled by their crews. Even at the end, there was something defiant (or proud?) about these men. Despite the fact that 630 U-boats had been lost at sea, and 30,000 men had been killed, the survivors had known success – and the taste of it had lingered. But the darkest hour for Doenitz came on 7 May 1945. As Hitler's appointed successor, it was he who had to haul down the flag of the Third Reich on VE–Day. His submarines had accounted for some 14·5 million tons of Allied shipping.[6] The war had cost him the lives of his two sons – and, as a result of the Nuremberg Tribunal, 10 years of his liberty. If only his advanced submarines had been ready earlier; if only Hitler had not derided the idea of radar ... Doenitz had plenty to think about during his second captivity.

A peaceful dawn breaks over an American convoy in the Atlantic, 1944. Germany is contemplating the building of the XXVI, but it is too late.

7 Trans-Pacific

The big submarine feature of the Second World War was staged on and in the Atlantic. It existed in its own right. The object was simple: to cut Britain off from all sources of supply. By comparison, submarine warfare in the Pacific is apt to be reduced to an historical footnote. In fact, this is unreasonable, for the United States Navy succeeded in doing what many others had hoped to do – and failed. By achieving considerable success, its submariners demonstrated that these boats could be used in collaboration with surface fleets – and that, in some circumstances, they could be more devastating than the warships themselves.

In December 1941, the Japanese had over 60 submarines, of which 42 were large vessels capable of crossing the Pacific. They appear to have been inspired partly by the British K class and partly by the *M2*. Not only were they required to serve as integral units in a fleet; they had also to transport weapons beyond the average submersible's capacity. Eleven of them had been built as carriers for small seaplanes; five acted as mother ships to midget submarines. All of them were slow to dive and unresponsive when submerged.

The Japanese submarine force was known as the Sixth Fleet, and was part of the combined fleet. Four of the boats were, indeed, fitted with special communication systems to enable them to function as flag ships. Their designers

PREVIOUS PAGES During the war in the Pacific, surface fleets collaborated with submarines – with devastating success.

BELOW Mother and child. The parent submarine, on passage from the Japanese naval base at Kure, carries a midget on her back. The deck is sloped to make the launching of the smaller vessel easier.

seem to have overlooked the fact that wireless was useless when the vessels were submerged – with the result that their admirals were seldom in touch. Attacks on merchant shipping had to be regarded as a second option – to be undertaken only if they had nothing better to do.

Midget submarines were by no means an impossibility. The Royal Navy used them to good effect against the German battleship *Tirpitz* – and, indeed, against the Japanese themselves, when the *XE1* and the *XE3* entered Singapore harbour and severely damaged the 9850-ton cruiser *Takoa*. In the attack on Pearl Harbor the Nippon High Command intended to give them an important role. It was even predicted that they would be more formidable than the carrier-borne aircraft. In the event, however, only one of them managed to penetrate into the roadstead, and that did virtually no damage. Before the day was over, all of them had been destroyed.

Three days after the main assault on Pearl Harbor, Japanese submarines made a second strike. One of them torpedoed the aircraft carrier *Saratoga*. The effect was to put her out of action at a time when she was badly needed. During the second half of 1942, in operations around Guadalcanal in the Solomon Islands, the *I.19* sank the aircraft carrier *Wasp*; the *I.15* damaged the battleship *North Carolina*; and the *I.26* hit the *Saratoga* (not long mended after her mis-

fortune near Hawaii) and sank the light cruiser *Juneau*. But this was the climax of an unremarkable saga. Never again did Japanese submarines inflict such damage and destruction. Indeed, many of them were eventually converted into supply ships. With one gun and two torpedoes removed, they could carry seventy tons – enough to support 13,000 men for two days. From November 1942, until February 1943, they made daily delivery trips to Guadalcanal.

It may seem surprising that the story of Japanese submarines in the Pacific was one of failure – while that of the United States's boats was successful. Both were large vessels designed for a similar purpose – that of crossing the ocean. During the early part of hostilities, the Americans – like the Germans – suffered the disadvantage of torpedoes that failed to explode. It took some time to discover the cause, which turned out to be faulty firing pins. One USN submarine, the *Sargo*, scored no fewer than eight hits on a carefully sighted target. Not one of them detonated.

Technically, the USN breed of submersibles grew into something vastly superior to anything the Japanese produced. But this was not the complete answer. Japan was, in many ways, comparable to Britain. As a collection of islands that depended on imports, she had more to fear than to gain from submarine warfare. Consequently, her navy was inclined to use the boats defensively. It was a purpose for which they were all too evidently unsuited.

BELOW LEFT The midget submarine is launched by gravity. The retaining blocks are removed, and it slides into the water over roller-bearings set between twin rails.

The probability of their being in the right place at the right time was remote; nor were they sufficiently agile to be used as a mobile reserve. No: the job of a submarine was to attack. The Germans realized this and so did the Americans. While Britain was not without success in this realm, it is by no means fortuitous that the greater part of her naval reputation in the Second World War developed from the actions of her surface vessels *against* U-boats. Safeguarding ocean lifelines was a British naval tradition. Preying on those of others was not; and that, ultimately, was the purpose of these boats.

Had the Japanese concentrated more on the construction of efficient escorts, they might have fared better. The price of this oversight was that American submarines enjoyed a faster turn of speed than their hunters – and that, before the war was over, Japanese destroyers were being sunk by USN boats at a rate out of all proportion to their score of submarines.

At the outbreak of war with Japan, the Allies had 70 submarines in the Pacific: 55 of them were American boats – 29 with the Asiatic Fleet based on the Philippines, the remainder with the Pacific Fleet at Hawaii. By a lucky coincidence, there were only 5 in port at the time of the attack on Pearl Harbor, and they escaped undamaged. Down at Sourabaya in the East Indies, the Dutch had 15 boats. For 20 years, the British had maintained 18 submarines in the Far East for just such an eventuality. By the time they were needed, however,

The Japanese 'I'-class submarines were large, as became vessels designed to cross the Pacific. They were, however, unsuited to a defensive role and were seldom in the right place at the right time.

The vessels are Japanese 'Koryu' submarines at the Imperial Naval Base at Kure. The boats, which were developed during the latter part of the Second World War, each carried a crew of five and two torpedoes.

they had all been withdrawn to the Mediterranean.

The inadequacy of the submarine in a defender's role became apparent soon after the Japanese offensive began. The American boats from the Asiatic Fleet tried to intercept the invasion force driving towards the Philippines. Operating in waters that were too shallow and hampered by defective torpedoes, they did small damage. Only three ships were hit, and none of them was of any consequence. Nevertheless, they distinguished themselves by performing two less orthodox actions. The USS *Spearfish* evacuated army and navy nurses and one civilian woman from the island of Corregidor. USS *Trout* removed gold ingots from the Bank of the Philippines to prevent their falling into Japanese hands.

Robbed of the Philippine base, the Asiatic Fleet moved to Australia. The Dutch lost 5 boats – 2 of them when the Japanese overran Sourabaya. The survivors were divided up among the Americans and the British, who were now using Ceylon as their headquarters for the Far East. When, in 1943, the Royal Navy was able to re-deploy submarines from the Mediterranean, the Dutch and British boats worked together in the Malacca Straits, harassing the Japanese sealink to Burma. The operations were valuable, if unspectacular. In 1944, they sank 24 ships totalling 48,000 tons – most of them by gunfire. The trouble was that few large targets presented themselves.

These men are doomed. Within a few hours they will plunge their midget submarines into the sides of enemy ships, thereby killing themselves as well. Before the suicide mission, there is a moment of glory as each receives a bunch of flowers and a citation parchment.

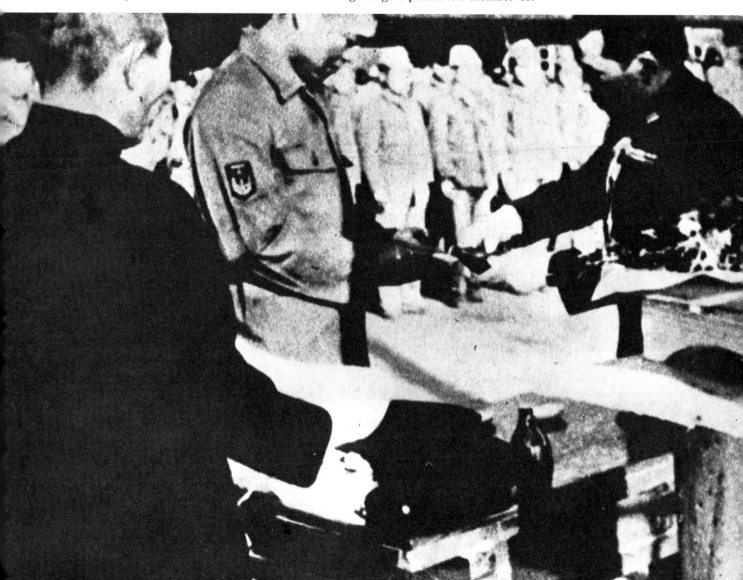

And the Japanese forces swept on, crossing the international date line, and eventually looming in sight of an isolated dot of land named Midway. The force was described in the *Biennial Report of the Chief of Staff of the United States Army* as 'the largest concentration of enemy strength yet assembled for Pacific operations'. The clash with the United States fleet occurred on 4 June 1942.

Part of the Japanese plan was to move 12 submarines to a point between Midway and Hawaii with the object of intercepting American reinforcements from Pearl Harbor. Somehow, the Americans received warning of this manoeuvre; the task force was diverted, and the submarine commanders never so much as glimpsed a target. Indeed, the entire contribution of Japanese boats to the Battle of Midway was the sinking of the US carrier *Yorktown* (already damaged) and her attendant destroyer, USS *Hammann*.

Midway marked a turning-point in two respects. It put an end to the Japanese advance across the long and empty expanse of the Pacific. It also signified the coming of age of American submarines. The days of defective torpedoes and apprenticeship in tactics were over. They knew what they had to do, and they did it very well. Indeed, the first report of that 'largest concentration of enemy strength' was received from the USS *Cuttlefish*, when the enemy units were still 700 miles away. Nine submarines from the group stationed at Midway were ordered to intercept. It may have been a defensive action, but it was carried out in an offensive manner. This was something that submariners understood. There was no question of hoping that the intended victims would come to them. They went out and found them.

The most successful of the nine was the 3960-ton *Nautilus*, a vessel armed with two 6-inch guns and six 21-inch torpedo tubes. *Nautilus* had been laid down as long ago as August 1927. She had cost the United States Treasury over $5 million. Now, she was to make handsome repayment by sinking the aircraft carrier *Soryu*. The USS *Tambor* also assured herself of immortality, though, it must be confessed, by accident. She was spotted by four heavy cruisers on their way to bombard the island. Two of them sheered off to attack; but, in the confusion, they made a fatal misjudgement. Instead of putting an end to the *Tambor*, they collided. The accident aborted their mission of bombardment. Eventually they were finished off by aircraft.

But Midway was only a beginning. The bulk of the Japanese losses was accounted for by aircraft. Nevertheless, the American submarines had accomplished more than the surface vessels. Throughout the engagement, the battleships, the cruisers, the destroyers of both sides did not fire a single shot at one another.

Many miles to the south of Midway, action was brewing up in the area of the Solomon Islands. It was here that the Japanese submarines made their final, fairly substantial, onslaught. Meanwhile, a force of United States boats had been busy off Truk in the Caroline Islands – the base that supported Japanese operations in the Solomons. All told, they sank 23 supply ships. By the end of 1942, US Navy submarines had sunk 2 cruisers, 1 seaplane carrier, 4 destroyers, 6 submarines, and a sizeable total of supply vessels. From time to time, boats of the Royal Navy had landed agents on the shores of occupied Europe. The USS *Argonaut* and the USS *Nautilus* established some sort of record in this respect when they put ashore 211 Marines on Makin in the Gilbert group of islands.

In 1943 the United States submarines began to fulfil the promise of which the previous year had given such ample indication. When the Italian armistice was signed in September, British boats were released from their duties in the Mediterranean and sent east to Ceylon. There were now few areas of the ocean in which a Japanese merchantman could sail with the certainty of completing her voyage. They were sunk on sight; the United States Navy never, at any time, questioned the right to do so. Considering that German failure to obey the Cruiser Rules had been the chief reason for the US coming into the First World

The view through the periscope of an American submarine just after a Japanese freighter has received a mortal wound from one of the boat's torpedoes.

War, the oversight may seem surprising. One suggested reason has been that fury over the attack on Pearl Harbor was so intense that it abolished any concept of mercy. A more likely explanation is that, in the Atlantic, the Germans had already buried this fragment of history. The Americans were merely subscribing to the new standards produced by total war.

Whatever the ethics, there was no argument about the statistics. During the latter part of 1943, American submarines based on Brisbane sank 52 merchant ships totalling 240,000 tons. The boats were also used to reconnoitre locations for beach landings, and to dispatch any Japanese ships that might seek to interfere with them. The USS *Skate* scored a hit on the giant battleship *Yamato*, but failed to sink her. The *Sailfish*, while on a routine patrol, was more successful when she destroyed the escort carrier *Chuyo* off the coast of Japan. During this period, the Japanese lost 23 submarines. Their only success was the sinking of the auxiliary carrier *Liscombe Bay*. But, by now, most of them had been converted into submersible supply vessels.

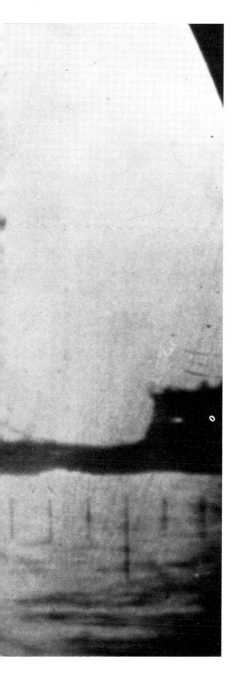

By the beginning of 1944, United States submarines were being employed in much the manner of the U-boat wolf-packs. Functioning in groups of seven, their object was to carry out patrols and to report movements of the Japanese fleet. While they were permitted to attack isolated units, their orders specified that they were not to engage large formations. One of the more spectacular actions was that of the USS *Harder*, when she sank four enemy destroyers. The technique used by *Harder*'s commanding officer was the so-called 'down the throat' method. It could be very effective – provided you had sufficient nerve.

The idea was to approach the enemy head on; then, at relatively close range, to fire a spread of torpedoes. Success was essential. If it failed, the loss of the submarine was almost certain. But, throughout the whole of 1944, the Japanese sank only six US boats. Indeed, in any action between a Nippon escort vessel and a submarine, the odds were now reckoned at three to one in the latter's favour.

In June 1944, an attack by the Americans on Saipan heralded the battle of the Philippine Sea. A force of 28 United States submarines was stationed in the vicinity – 3 of them off the vital Japanese oil base at Tawi Tawi in the Philippines. It was these vessels that alerted the American formations when the enemy fleet came out to do battle. Four boats attempted to intercept the warships while they were refuelling, but presently they lost contact. The USS *Cavalla* and the USS *Albacore* were more successful, when they sighted the main Japanese carrier force. The *Cavalla* promptly sank the *Shokakku* – shortly afterwards, the *Albacore* put an end to the brief life of the newly completed *Taiho*. A third carrier was sunk by aircraft. For the first time, United States submarines had accounted for as many enemy warships as the combined forces of aircraft and surface ships.

Four months later, the United States invasion of Leyte in the Philippines began. All told, there were 36 submarines at sea – some carrying out normal patrols against commerce, others on the alert to cover actions against the Japanese fleet. In the shooting match that followed, the USS *Dace* and the USS *Darter* sank the heavy cruisers *Atago* and *Maya*, which were part of a formation steaming up from the south under the command of Admiral Kurita. The *Atago* was, as it happened, the admiral's flag ship. All his communications staff went down with her; Kurita transferred his flag to another cruiser, but the confusion caused by the sinking did little to assist the Japanese thrust. All told, USN submarines sank five cruisers and a destroyer. What was more, they were able to report the movements of enemy ships beyond the range of aircraft reconnaissance. The dream conceived by Lord Jellicoe all those many years ago had achieved reality. Submarines had at last become an important faction in fleet engagements.

As the Japanese withdrew to the South China Sea, the killings continued. The USS *Sealion* sank the battleship *Kongo* and her escort destroyer. Four boats drove the heavy cruiser *Kumano* ashore on the Philippines (the *coup de grâce* was administered by aircraft). In November, the *Archerfish* sank the recently completed carrier *Shinano* off the coast of Japan. Among other victims was the light cruiser *Kuma*, which fell to the British submarine *Tally Ho* in the Malacca Straits, and the heavy cruiser *Ashigara* – dispatched by the Royal Navy's *Trenchant*.

By now, it seemed almost too easy. Naval history was becoming, simply, a list of the sinkers and the sunk – a collection of names that looked as if it had been torn out of a copy of *Jane's Fighting Ships*. It becomes, perhaps, more remarkable when one considers that, at the end of the war, these vessels accounted for only two per cent of American forces in the Pacific. All told, submarines belonging to the United States Navy sank a total of 5·5 million tons of Japanese shipping – and this was not their only achievement. At one time or another, they rescued 380 aviators from the ocean.

This Japanese two-man midget submarine once set off on a mission of destruction. Now, with her stern blown off, she lies abandoned on a Pacific Island.

There were, of course, some occasions that astonished by their sheer audacity. In this respect, the top award must be given to Lieut. Chester Smith of the United States Navy. Lieut. Smith had the temerity to take his submarine into Tokyo harbour, where he sank a heavily escorted 17,000-ton ship. Having accomplished his mission, he withdrew to the safety of the ocean. After such an achievement, one does not hang around hoping for applause. The last torpedo of the war was fired by the Royal Navy's HMS *Statesman*, but it was not discharged in anger. The victim was a derelict Japanese vessel that had become a hazard to navigation.

Perhaps there was something appropriate about the conclusion of the Pacific war. The genesis of the submarine owed a great deal to that American inventor, John Philip Holland. Having set the world's navies on to the right paths of development, the United States seemed to withdraw. Even their most fervent friends could find little to applaud in the belated and ineffective attempts to wage underwater warfare during the First World War. But, at the conclusion of the second great clash of arms, there was much to admire. The U-boats, for all

the valour of their crews, had set themselves against the supine shapes of merchantmen. When confronted by adequate escort forces equipped with the latest anti-submarine devices, Admiral Doenitz was compelled to capitulate his command of the Atlantic. But the United States submarines pitched themselves into the fray against the cream of the Japanese Navy – and won. If the late Lord Jellicoe could have seen it from his command post in the sky, he would have been delighted. It was exactly what he had hoped submarines would be able to accomplish.

8 Nuclear

At about the time Helmuth Walther was carrying out experiments into the possibility of using highly concentrated hydrogen peroxide as a means of submarine propulsion, an American named Ross Gunn was pursuing an even more original line of research. Gunn's idea was to employ nuclear fission. A reactor would generate steam, which would drive a turbine. Dr Walther's engine was able to produce high speeds under water, but only for comparatively short periods. In theory at any rate, there need be no such restriction with a nuclear power plant. As Gunn reported in 1939, his brainchild would 'enormously increase the range and military effectiveness of a submarine.'

There, for the time being, matters had to rest. All the United States's efforts in the nuclear field were directed towards the development of an atomic bomb, and little more was heard from Gunn until the end of the war. By this time he had teamed up with Philip Abelson of the Carnegie Institute. In the spring of 1946, the two men produced a second document urging the US Navy to experiment with a nuclear submarine. The Navy Department did its best to shrug the project off, but a new character was about to come on to the scene. His name was Captain Hyman G. Rickover, USN, an officer whose store of enthusiasm seemed unbounded. Captain Rickover was appointed to head up a naval team cooperating in a nuclear project at the Oak Ridge, Tennessee research centre. Inevitably he heard about the work of Gunn and Abelson; and, equally inevitably, it fired his imagination. The two men now had a powerful and articulate ally. The result was that the Navy Department agreed to the building of a land-based prototype plant. Shortly afterwards, a duplicate was ordered. It was to be installed in USS *Nautilus*, the world's first nuclear submarine.

On a day in June 1952, President Harry S. Truman signed his name on a metal plate incorporated into the hull of *Nautilus*. She was ready for trials by the beginning of 1955; on 17 January her commanding officer, Commander E. P. Wilkinson, sent the historic signal; 'Under way on nuclear power.' The attitude to submarines would never be the same again.

In appearance, the most advanced underwater ship in the world was much like a conventional submarine. But thereafter any similarity ended. All previous vessels, even those equipped with schnorkels, had really been submersibles. When they surfaced, one felt that they were grateful to return to the world above. *Nautilus* was different. Listed as an 'attack submarine', she could cruise at the then remarkable speed of 20 knots submerged. Nor did she hanker after fresh air; she was prepared to remain in the depths of the ocean for as long as anyone wished (or almost). Rightly and with great enthusiasm, her admirers described her as 'the first true submarine'.

Presently *Nautilus* gave the world evidence of her capabilities. Early in her career, she travelled submerged from the naval base at New London, Connecticut to Puerto Rico and back. The distance was getting on for 3000 miles. Nothing like it had ever been seen before. But this was only a beginning. In 1958, she achieved the amazing feat of crossing from Point Barrow, Alaska, to the Greenland Sea. The distance was 1830 miles; during the trip she passed beneath the North Pole. In the same year, her sister – USS *Skate* – rose up through the ice to surface at a point 40 miles from the pole. Since then other nuclear submarines have performed similar feats. The art, it seems, is to come up vertically, with no head- or stern-way on the ship, probing through a 'polynia' – a word coined by the Russians for a space of open water amid the ice. 'However,' a United States naval officer told the author, 'the submarines can force their way through a limited thickness of ice.'

At least three vessels – one American, one British, and one Russian – have surfaced at the pole itself. This is very spectacular. In practical terms, the ability to travel beneath the Arctic ice creates two advantages. One is that the ocean's roof of ice provides cover against surface and airborne anti-submarine detec-

PREVIOUS PAGES The first of a new generation of submarines, USS *Nautilus* pioneered the road leading to nuclear vessels. She is seen here in New York harbour after her historic voyage beneath the North Pole.

OPPOSITE HMS *Resolution* carrying sixteen missiles, each with a 30,000-mile range, puts out to sea.

The officers of USS *Nautilus* after her trip to Pearl Harbour via the North Pole; the flag commemorates her achievement.

tion equipment. The other is that distances have become dramatically reduced. As *Nautilus* demonstrated when, again in 1958, she travelled from Hawaii to England via the ice cap, the shortest distance from the Pacific to Europe is by way of the North Pole. Similarly, a British nuclear submarine could journey from England to Singapore, remain a month on patrol in the Far East, and return to her home port – spending only three months at sea. The attack submarine HMS *Valiant* has already demonstrated the feasibility of this by making the journey from Singapore in 28 days non-stop. This still stands as the record for a submerged passage by a UK submarine.

With a displacement of 3539 tons on the surface (4092 submerged), *Nautilus* was larger than any previous submarine. Her armament amounted to 6 forward torpedo tubes and a stock of 20 homing torpedoes. She was also equipped with unusually sensitive sonar apparatus (in Britain, often referred to as 'asdic'). The moment she arrived on the scene, all existing anti-submarine techniques became obsolete. Indeed, with her high performance underwater, she promised to outdate destroyers and frigates as the conventional escorts of surface ships.

Nuclear power meant that a submarine could live beneath the surface for an almost indefinite length of time. Having achieved this, it was possible to take a fresh look at the vessels themselves. With their dual lives above and below the waves, the old boats had been a compromise. Like most attempts to fulfil two

purposes with one object, they were not entirely satisfactory. For example, a pointed bow was needed for cruising on the surface. Consequently, the ballast had to be contained in saddle tanks on either side of the hull. The shape was far from streamlined, but there appeared to be no alternative.

Once the need for surface travel had been removed, all sorts of things became possible. For example, the saddle tanks could be done away with: compartments at the front and the rear of the vessel could be used instead. Such a major modification would produce streamlining – and with it would come even more speed. The first steps in this direction were taken by scientists working at the Davis Taylor Model Basin in America. Presently, an experimental boat named the *Albacore* was built. She was powered by electric motors, but that was simply a matter of economy. What mattered was the shape of her hull. It was shortish and plump – rather like a tear drop. She was powered by a single screw abaft the rudder. The only protrusions were planes (used for ascending, descending and maintaining what, in aircraft terms, would be called level flight), and the conning tower (soon to be referred to as the 'sail' in the USA; as the 'fin' in Britain). Some observers likened her appearance to that of a whale. It was not an unreasonable description. If one ignores a submarine's armament, the designers of both had similar ideas in mind.

The first operational submarine to benefit from the work on *Albacore* was

The introduction of nuclear power meant that the true submarine had arrived at last. It could now spend all its time submerged. The USS *Albacore* carried the revolution a stage further by employing a new concept of hull design.

HMS *Resolution* displaces 7,000 tons, has four decks, two crews, and enjoys almost unlimited endurance sea.

LEFT USS *Whale* surfaces at the North Pole, 6 April 1969.

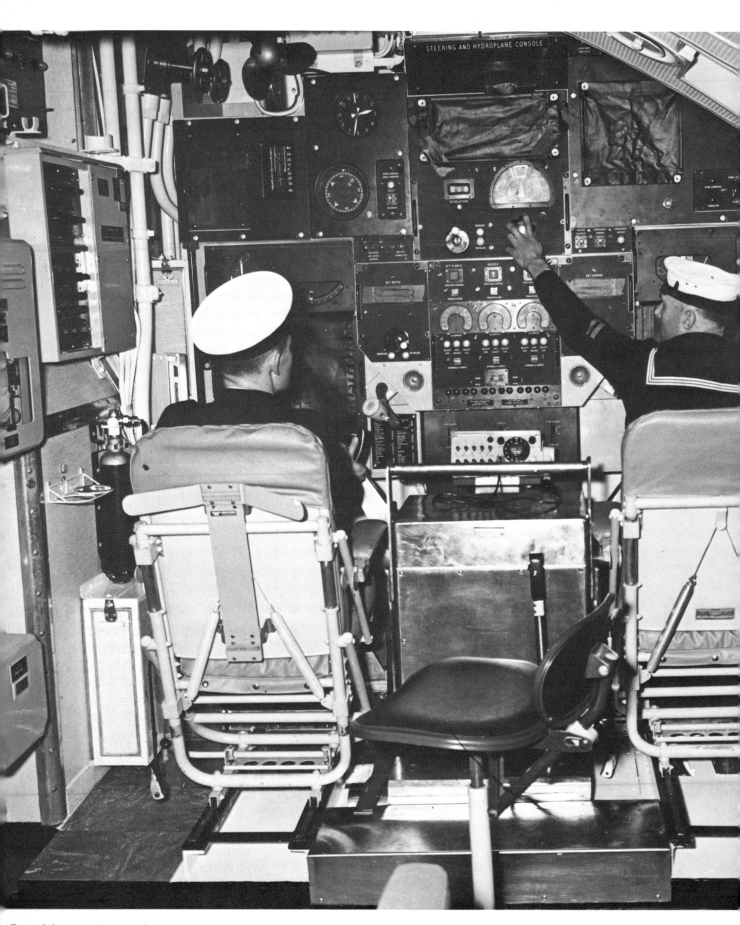

Part of the control room of HMS
Dreadnought. The petty officer on the left
is conning the ship; the rating beside him
is operating the hydroplane.

the USS *Skipjack*. Her performance on trials was described as 'sensational', and the underwater revolution was almost complete. By 1960, the United States had 15 nuclear boats and another 14 under construction. The building of conventional vessels had ceased altogether.

One of the less enviable tasks of surface ships had been to act as radar pickets. They were stationed well ahead of the main fleet, with the object of establishing an advanced screen to give warning of enemy movements. They were unprotected and, therefore, extremely vulnerable. This duty now fell within the scope of a submarine, and the USS *Triton* was designed for just such a purpose. Completed in 1959 and equipped with two nuclear reactors, she was a large vessel displacing 5963 tons on the surface (7773 submerged). Eventually in 1961 she was re-classified as an attack submarine; but before that she had secured herself a place in history. In 1960, she produced an underwater version of Jules Verne's epic by going round the world in 80 days. In fact, she did it in rather less. The actual circumnavigation began and ended at a point in mid-Atlantic, and was accomplished in 60 days. The distance was 36,000 miles: at no point did the *Triton* surface.

Although, for a good many years after the last war, British submarine construction was devoted to conventional vessels, the Admiralty was concerned about the shape of future developments. Between 1939 and 1945, boats belonging to the Royal Navy had sunk 40 German, Italian and Japanese submarines – but mostly on the surface, and then almost as a sideline. It now became clear that like would have to fight against like – that one of a submarine's prime tasks would be to attack its own species. With the advances in technology, the conventional diesel-electric boats had obvious limitations.

At the end of the war, one of Dr Walther's smaller boats, the *U1407*, was taken over by the British Navy and renamed HMS *Meteorite*. This led to the construction of two experimental submarines, HMS *Explorer* and HMS *Excalibur*. Like *Meteorite*, they were powered by concentrated hydrogen peroxide. They were certainly an improvement. Nevertheless, in terms of performance, they had few of the virtues associated with nuclear vessels, and they were extremely expensive. In 1955, this line of research was abandoned, and the building of a nuclear submarine was authorized. The power plant was purchased from America; the hull was designed along the lines of *Skipjack*; and, not without significance, the vessel was named HMS *Dreadnought*. She became operational in 1963. By calling her *Dreadnought*, the Admiralty seemed to acknowledge the fact that the submarine had graduated from corsair to capital ship. It was the nation's first line of defence – and, if need be, the vanguard of attack.

In 1953, the USSR added several more worry lines to the foreheads of the Western powers by exploding an atomic bomb. Five years later, she produced a nuclear-powered ice-breaker for service in the Arctic. It would obviously not be long before a nuclear submarine followed. The newcomer arrived in 1959 (the exact date is uncertain; it may have been 1960) in the shape of a clutch of *November* class boats. Armed with six torpedo tubes in the bows, they had a speed of 25 knots on the surface, and between 25 and 30 submerged. At about this time, Russian naval strategy seems to have undergone a disturbing change of emphasis. Previously, its submarine arm had appeared to be playing a defensive role – that of keeping any United States strike force at a respectful distance from the Norwegian Sea. But now, as Soviet submarines began to make longer voyages, the prospect of a more offensive policy had to be considered.

By 1956, the United States had developed a missile known as the Regulus. It was on the lines of the German V-1 rocket that had been used to bombard London during the Second World War – except that, unlike the V-1, it was fitted with a nuclear warhead. Its range was limited to a few hundred miles. The USS *Halibut* was built to carry several of them, but, initially, only one per submarine could be transported – and, even in *Halibut*'s case, it was necessary

The launch of HMS *Dreadnought*: the birth
of Britain's nuclear submarine age.

The Dreadnought

BELOW HM the Queen presides over the launch of *Dreadnought*.

BELOW RIGHT The hull of *Dreadnought* was not unlike that of the USS *Skipjack* whose power plant design she duplicated.

RIGHT 'Fixing the ship' whilst at sea, from the bridge in the conning tower.

CENTRE At the search periscope.

FAR RIGHT *Dreadnought* at sea, the ninth Royal Navy ship to bear the name.

Although the ability to travel under the ice was the important advance in submarine development, the USS *Whale* surfacing through an Arctic polnya demonstrates another phase of the adventure.

The Regulus, similar to the V1 rockets that bombed London during the Second World War, was the first ballistic missile to be launched from a submarine. The target is 200 miles away; the launching pad is the USS *Grayback*.

to surface before they could be fired. At best, a Regulus could wipe out an enemy naval base from comparatively close quarters.

The coming of the Jupiter missile produced the first of the inter-continental weapons; but it was 60 feet long and driven by extremely volatile liquid fuel. It had the range and its destructive power was terrible, but it was completely unsuitable for carrying in a submarine. Indeed, the idea was so far-fetched that it was not even attempted.

For as long as NATO had the monopoly of nuclear weapons, there was little cause for alarm in the West. The explosion of the Russian nuclear device in 1953 completely changed the picture. The two sides were not yet evenly matched, but that condition was not far off. The possibilities were fearful. If one side or the other made a pre-emptive strike, it had to be assumed that the victim's airfields and missile bases would be put out of action immediately. Once this had happened, there could be no retaliation – and, without it, no deterrent. The only possible solution seemed to be the submarine. It was unseen. It would be immune from any holocaust on land, and it was extremely mobile. Such features made it an ideal launching platform for a counterstrike. Such was the American viewpoint; the Russians saw two further advantages. The journey from Eastern Europe to the United States and back was beyond the range of even its largest bombers – and it had not yet produced an intercontinental missile that could reach North America.

The immediate problem was to develop a missile that a nuclear submarine could carry – and which it could fire from beneath the surface. The breakthrough came in the late 1950s when the United States produced the Polaris. It was only 28 feet long, weighed 28,000 lb, and was powered by solid fuel. The original version – the Polaris A-1 – had a range of 1200 nautical miles. In 1958, an attack submarine – due to be named USS *Scorpion* – was under construction. Work on her was suddenly halted; her partially completed hull was cut open, and a missile section, 130 feet long, was inserted in the centre. The vessel was renamed USS *George Washington*. On 20 July 1960, she fired the first Polaris test vehicle from under water off Cape Canaveral. Three hours later, she fired a second. Both performances were satisfactory.

George Washington and her successors have all carried 16 missiles.[7] In the intervening years, both the ships and the weapons have developed. The A-2 Polaris extended the range to 1500 nautical miles, and the A-3 added another 1000 miles. Each is 31 feet long and weighs 30,000 lb. They are launched from tubes in the submarine's side by means of gas or air ejectors. As soon as they reach the surface, the rocket motor ignites and a method known as inertial guidance homes them on to their targets. It is similar to SINS (Ship's Inertial Navigation System), which is among the navigational aids installed in the vessel herself. The missile's course is related to the submarine's position, the trajectory, the location of the target, and true north. Like SINS, which relates the movements of the submarine to her speed over the ocean floor and true north, it emits no radio waves. The missile can only be detected by radar.

More recently, the Polaris family has been extended by the Poseidon – 34 feet long, 60,000 lb at launching and also with a range of 2500 miles. It can, however, cover a greater spread of targets.

The world's first Polaris submarine was the USS *George Washington*, seen here at the missile-loading facility, Charleston, North Carolina. A 30-ft cartridge is being lowered into one of the tubes as part of a demonstration.

ABOVE An impression of one of the US Navy's deep submergence rescue vehicles in operation.

RIGHT The deep submergence rescue vehicle undergoing tests on the USS *Skipjack*.

The creation of the *George Washington* was a somewhat extempore business, but it worked well enough. A number of other vessels were built in the class – all of them enlarged *Skipjacks* – until presently they made way for the Ethan Allen submarines. Displacing 6950 tons (7900 submerged), five of this type were built. They provided improved accommodation for their crews, but they were transitional. In the 1961 fiscal year, the US Government authorized the building of four fleet ballistic missile submarines belonging to the Lafayette class. The cost of each was $109,500,000 – the nuclear cores, which provide sufficient energy for about four hundred thousand miles, set the Treasury back about $3·5 million apiece.

A Lafayette class submarine displaces 7300 tons on the surface, and 8250 submerged. She has a speed of over 30 knots under water; her complement amounts to 17 officers and 128 enlisted men. The only comparable vessels are those in the USSR's Delta class, which first came off the slipways in November 1973. Registering 8000 tons on the surface and 9000 under water, the Russian ships are equipped with 12 missiles (later versions may have 16) plus 8 21-inch torpedo tubes. The latest missile, the SS-NX-18, is believed to have a range of about 4,600 miles – considerably more than the Polaris or the Poseidon.

Britain's original nuclear deterrent was a device named 'Thor', which was purchased from the USA. In the late 1950s, trying to achieve self-sufficiency, the government authorized work on a project known as 'Blue Streak'. A rocket was built; but, before it could be introduced as a weapons system, it was abandoned. The buying agents went back across the Atlantic; they looked with interest at an airborne strike missile called 'Skybolt', and reached for their order forms. But this, too, was cancelled.

The fact of the matter was that, as a launching platform for missiles, Britain was too small. Even if the silos were situated underground, a thermo-nuclear attempt to neutralize them would probably destroy most of the country. The aerodromes would certainly be among the casualties. Once the V-bombers were out of action, 'Skybolt' would be useless. Since it was also extremely expensive, some other method of second strike had to be found.

At last, in 1962, the situation stabilized itself at a meeting in Nassau between President Kennedy and Prime Minister Harold Macmillan. Kennedy agreed to supply technical know-how for the building of Polaris submarines. The result was that, in the following year, the British government decided to build four of these ships.

The specifications for the quartet, which was completed between 1967 and 1969, listed a length of 425 feet and a displacement of about 7000 tons. Although their design was clearly influenced by the American Polaris submarines, they were indigenous British products – even down to the warheads on their missiles (though the missiles themselves were purchased from the United States).

As on the American vessels, the British employ two crews. The idea is that the submarines can remain in commission almost continuously – with one set of personnel on board, the other either training or on leave. The United States Navy calls them 'Blue and Gold'; the Royal Navy, 'Port and Starboard'. An American patrol lasts for 60 days – after which the submarine spends 28 days alongside the Polaris tender. The duration of a British patrol is anything up to 10 weeks – or even longer, depending on the vessel's maintenance requirements.

Nowadays, Britain has a fleet of four ballistic missile submarines: HMS *Resolution*, HMS *Renown*, HMS *Repulse* and HMS *Revenge*. Like the *Dreadnought*, they are all named after former battleships and battle cruisers.

Predictably, France – the fourth nuclear submarine power – decided to go it alone. In the early 1960s, having exploded its first atomic bomb, the French government announced plans to create an independent counterstrike force. It was to be called a *force de frappe*, though it is also known – more appropriately,

perhaps, as a *force de dissuasion*. Eventually, there were to be between three and five Polaris-type vessels. The trouble was that, for the time being, there were no nuclear submarines from which to launch the missiles. Consequently, the early tests were conducted from conventional boats.

France had, in fact, begun work on a nuclear submarine in 1958. It was to be called the *Q244*; but, suddenly, it was cancelled. Six years later, in 1964, a vessel named *Redoutable* was laid down. She was completed in 1969, and became the first of France's present-day fleet of four ballistic missile ships. At about the same time as *Redoutable* was under construction, the first French nuclear attack submarine, the *Rubis*, was also being built.

Members of the Royal Navy's submarine service are all volunteers: there are, it seems, no problems concerning the morale of crews serving for long periods submerged. However, a contributor to an issue of *US Naval Institute Proceedings* published in 1967 gave a disturbing view of life in a SSBN (fleet ballistic missile submarine). According to him, the captains of these ships were men who had enjoyed successful careers in either diesel-electric vessels, or else in nuclear attack submarines. They and their chief engineers had undergone a year's special nuclear schooling and prototype training. The officers in the weapons and navigating departments, on the other hand, received no special instruction. The writer referred to 'a very boring and unchanging routine'. After a few years in SSBN submarines, junior officers began to 'feel stifled', and yet they were serving in a branch of the Navy demanding 'constant vigilance, intelligence and dedication'. Attack submarines were busy seeking out the enemy, but missile vessels had no such variety. Their job was to avoid any encounter; to remain unseen in the dark world of inner space. Such a situation, obviously, created monotony.

A spokesman for the United States Navy agreed that 'long periods of submersion can affect crew morale and efficiency'. Nowadays, however, a great deal is done to overcome the monotony. In terms of entertainment, a different motion picture is shown on every evening of the patrol; a coinless juke box emits the latest hit tunes; and a supply of video-taped TV programmes is available for transmission on the closed-circuit television system. Each of the submarines has a 'health room' – equipped with weight-lifting apparatus and other aids to exercise. About the only recreation that is not allowed is gambling. Many of the men, however, devote their off-duty hours to university and high school correspondence courses. The food is described as 'famous for its quality, quantity and availability'. The two favourite items on the menus are steak and lobster.

The story of submarines is largely one of evolution. Attempts to produce breakaway ideas during and after the First World War were almost all failures. Indeed, until the coming of nuclear power and the 'tear-drop' concept of hull design, the shape of these vessels changed very little in nearly half a century.

Undoubtedly, the use of nuclear power has produced an entirely new concept – even a new type of warship. One day, the United States intends to introduce what may be the ultimate missile submarine – until something even more ultimate arises from a drawing-board. Known as the Trident class, these vessels will carry weapons that will, in the Trident II D–5, ultimately have a range of about 6000 miles. Classified as MIRV (multiple independently targeted re-entry vehicles), they will afford a much wider range of targeting options against the USSR. The ships will be equipped to fire 24 of them – 8 more than the present *Polaris* submarines. Predictably, the vessels will be larger than ever – displacing 12,000 tons on the surface, 15,000 submerged.

The original idea was to produce three a year. Since then, the programme has been revised. Even if the present schedule is honoured, the tenth *Trident* will not be in service until 1985. The problems are the huge costs and the limited shipbuilding facilities for nuclear vessels. The danger is that, by the time

OPPOSITE Unseen beneath the surface of the ocean, a United States' nuclear submarine engages another submarine. When it re-enters the water the missile will detonate and produce a nuclear explosion. The system is known as SUBROC.

PREVIOUS PAGES
The missile compartment of Britain's Polaris submarine, HMS *Resolution*.

they are ready, more advanced detection systems may have already rendered them vulnerable. In any case, it seems probable that the range of the Trident I missile (between 3000 and 4000 miles) has already been exceeded by the SS–NX–18 carried by Soviet Delta submarines.

At present, the most advanced Russian submarine operating in any quantity seems to be the Yankee class (in Western circles, the various types are known by letters in the phonetic alphabet; if they do have individual names, they are kept secret). Initially, they were deployed off the eastern seaboard of the United States – covering an area northwards of the Mississippi. More recently, however, they are known to have crossed the Pacific. They are, it is suspected, patrolling from California to a point seaward of the Rocky Mountains. According to one estimate, there are 33 Yankee class boats in service – the total submarine strength of all four Red fleets is about 390.[8] The United States have 41 ballistic missile submarines and 64 attack submarines.

Britain's second Polaris submarine, *Renown*, launched in 1967.

The difference between an attack submarine and a missile vessel is, in some respects, a matter of size. The latter are much larger, since they have to accommodate the silos from which the weapons are launched. Otherwise, they have many features in common; and, after suitable training, the crews are interchangeable. The largest attack (fleet) submarines will soon be those of America's Los Angeles class – displacing 6900 tons submerged. Their armament will include anti-submarine and anti-surface ship torpedoes, 'Harpoon' missiles for use against surface vessels, and SUBROC ASW missiles for use against other submarines. The last of these is equipped with a nuclear warhead. When it is fired, it rises to the surface – and detonates on re-entry into the sea. The range is between 25 and 30 miles.

No two submarines are identical. A fairly typical example of a British fleet submarine is HMS *Courageous*. She displaces more than a frigate – and only slightly less than a guided missile destroyer. On the rare occasions when she is to be seen on the surface, she draws 30 feet – which is comparable to the draught of a fleet aircraft carrier or the *QEII*. But the only times that she is in this situation are when she is entering or leaving harbour. Throughout her patrols of up to 10 weeks, she is submerged – often at depths of 500 feet or more. In these regions of the sea, there is no turbulence and almost absolute silence. The result is that her sonar and other sensor equipment can function at its maximum efficiency. It is possible to detect the sound of waves breaking on a beach 100 miles away. Not only can it locate surface vessels and other submarines – it can even identify their types.

Courageous's speed under water is in excess of 25 knots, and she is extremely manoeuvrable. In some respects, she might be likened to a giant aircraft; there are planes near the bow and at the after end, and two large rudders which work together. When executing a tight turn, she is apt to bank in the manner of an aeroplane – to such an extent that some of the men at the controls have to be strapped into their seats.

In the pre-nuclear submarines, a great deal of effort had to be expended on the conservation of water and electricity. It was, in theory, possible to distil seawater; but this required power – which meant further demands on the batteries. The use of turbo-generators has created a situation in which a vessel such as *Courageous* generates enough electricity to supply a town of 40,000 inhabitants. Distillation is the least of the problems; indeed, among the facilities for the comfort of her crew, there are shower baths and a launderette.

A vital part of a nuclear submariner's life is an art known as 'atmosphere control'. Oxygen is supplied by an electrolyzer, which extracts it from seawater. If there were too much of it, the crew would achieve a state of euphoria – if there were too little, they would become drowsy. It has to be nicely balanced. Air scrubbers remove undesirable gases such as carbon dioxide and carbon monoxide. In the engineering compartments occupying the after part of the hull, the men wear radiation badges. The amount absorbed is small – less, probably, than the average citizen soaks up when walking along an urban street.

The vessel is crammed with fail-safe devices – such as oxygen candles, which produce a very acceptable alternative to the electrolysis method. In the case of a breakdown in the engine-room, it is possible to drive the submarine by diesel-electric propulsion (re-creating all the old snags of this method), and the chances of a nuclear explosion simply do not exist. The worst that could happen is that the reactor's core might become over-heated and degenerate into a kind of molten isotope. But this has never happened in the Navy's 14 years of nuclear submarine experience. Indeed, the safeguards are so effective, that the possibility of an occurrence is reckoned to be once in 10,000 years.

On patrols, the routine varies according to the commanding officer. Movies are provided on the assumption that they are a quick and easy form of relaxation. In fact, the men are extremely busy. Once they have come off watch, they are largely preoccupied with such basic functions as eating and sleeping. The menus vary from one submarine to another. In *Courageous*, they always have roast beef on Sundays – steaks and scampi are also popular. One galley services the whole ship, and the fare is the same in the officers' ward-room as it is on the lower deck. After three weeks at sea, the cooks must resort to frozen vegetables; after five, they bake their own bread. Taking on food for a patrol is, somebody has estimated, equivalent to shopping for a family of four over a period of six years – though, unlike this hypothetical household, it is impossible to nip round to the supermarket if anything has been forgotten. Were it not for the fact that she would one day run out of food, a fleet submarine could remain at sea more or less forever.

During the patrols, the only thing that distinguishes day from night is that, when the world above becomes dark, the lights in the control room and in the officers' quarters are switched over to red. The reason is that it assists the men's vision if the periscope has to be used. Otherwise, periods of time are marked by such things as the Sunday roast, a regular church service, or whatever – small events that break the monotony of routine.

Strangely enough, this world, in which there is so little to denote the passage of days, does not disorientate its inhabitants. However, when they come ashore, many of them find that their eyes have been affected by looking at objects that, in the cramped confines of the ship's four decks, are never more than 12 feet away. It becomes difficult to judge distances, and they are advised not to drive a car until they have had 24 hours in which to adjust. There was even a case in which a submarine officer had to be helped across the road on his first day ashore. He could not judge the distance nor the speed of the traffic.

But, despite these snags, the crew of an attack submarine seem a contented bunch of men. They are extremely proud of their ships, which they regard (rightly) as deterrents against aggression and as 'the main striking power of the fleet'. Navigation is by SINS – though, at intervals of two days or so, they come up to periscope depth to check their positions by means of a satellite (there are, in fact, six satellites for this purpose). The method is accurate to within 50 yards.

The old days, when a submarine submerged was out of contact with the rest of the world, are over. The breakthrough in this respect was produced by ultra low frequency radio which can pierce the stubborn silence of the sea. It is, however, largely a one-way system. The vessel is constantly receiving signals, but she seldom replies to them. To do so would be to give away her position; and thereby destroy the secrecy on which her mission depends.

Unlike the USN, the Royal Navy has not invested in the SUBROC weapon system. Until recently, the service continued to rely on the 21-inch torpedoes used in the Second World War. The reason was simple: nothing better had been produced. However, attack submarines are now equipped with 'wire guided' versions, which are steered by electric impulses to within a short distance of their targets – after which they automatically home on them. The Mk 24 torpedo, which is currently being issued, has been described as 'the finest torpedo in the world'. It is more akin to a guided missile than to a traditional torpedo.

There were many who believed that the outcome of the First World War would be decided by surface vessels – notably by capital ships. The result of the second was very largely determined by air power. The third, if there should ever be one, may be won or lost by submarines. Command of the skies becomes less important as the strike power from within the oceans increases. Surface warships are still necessary – to show the flag in places where the flag should be shown, and for deployment in smaller conflicts, where the use of a nuclear submarine's formidable weaponry would be excessive. In a major war, however, surface vessels will never again be the Navy's front line.

During the 70-odd years of this century the submarine has emerged from the unreliable, and often unpopular, hanger-on of navies, to the supreme deterrent.

The United States used to name these vessels after fish. Nowadays, the missile submarines carry the names of national heroes from George Washington downwards. British submarines – Polaris and fleet alike – are named after long departed battleships and battle cruisers. *Valiant* and *Warspite, Courageous* and *Conqueror, Swiftsure* and *Sovereign* – nominally, at least, they all have distinguished pedigrees. Conditions have changed. Commanders-in-chief no longer display their flags on giant warships; they plan and execute their tactics on land – working from operations rooms in bunkers. The onslaught, if it comes, will emerge from the dark and silent deep. In the final fury, the world will never see what hit it. But this is to take a pessimistic view. The nuclear submarine, with its power to strike back, is, perhaps, a guarantee of survival.

ABOVE HMS *Resolution*, seen here during the trial stages of fitting out, successfully fired her test Polaris missile at Cape Kennedy in 1968.

OVERLEAF HMS *Revenge*, Britain's fourth nuclear powered submarine at the commissioning ceremony.

Notes

1. Britain's first submarine casualty was the *A1*, which was lost with all hands in 1904 after being run down by a liner in Southampton Water.
2. *The World Crisis, 1911–1918.*
3. Theories about the *Bremen*'s fate vary. According to most accounts, she was lost with all hands. However, in *Warships of World War I*, H. M. Le Fleming reports that she was damaged and converted to a surface vessel.
4. On one of his very few trips afloat, the Führer had been violently seasick.
5. British submarines were more effective in this theatre of operations. They caused heavy losses among the ships supplying Rommel's Afrika Korps – a factor that contributed substantially to their defeat.
6. British submarines sank 1,520,000 tons of merchant shipping and 169 warships in all theatres of war. Seventy-four UK submarines were destroyed.
7. Estimated as a fire power greater than that of all the explosives used by all sides in the Second World War – including the two atomic bombs dropped on Japan.
8. This figure includes 204 conventional, diesel-electric boats.

Further Reading

Bekker, Cajus. *Hitler's Naval War* (Hamburg, 1971)
Carr, William Guy. *By Guess and by God* (London, 1930)
Churchill, Winston S. *The World Crisis*, Vols I and II (London, 1923)
Doenitz, Karl. *Memoirs* (London, 1959)
Everitt, Don. *The K-Boats* (London, 1963)
Hezlet, Arthur. *The Submarine and Sea Power* (London, 1967)
Jameson, William. *The Most Formidable Thing* (London, 1965)
Lipscomb, F. W. *The British Submarine* (London, 1954; rev. edn. 1975)
Mason, David. *U-Boat, the Secret Menace* (New York and London, 1968)
Roskill, S. W. *The Navy at War* (London, 1960)
Sueter, Murray F. *The Evolution of the Submarine Boat* (Portsmouth, 1907)
Sweeney, James B. *A Pictorial History of Ocean Submersibles* (London, 1972)
Werner, Herbert A. *Iron Coffins* (London, 1970)
Whitehouse, Arch. *Subs and Submariners* (London, 1963)

Acknowledgements

The illustrations in this book are supplied by or reproduced by kind permission of the following:

Bildarchiv Preussischer Kulturbesitz, Berlin *38–9*, *42–3*, *47* (bottom right), *64–5*, *back jacket*; Daily Telegraph Colour Library (Anthony Howarth), London *117*, *front jacket*; Fuji Photos, Tokyo 98–9, 100, 104, 108–9; Richard Garrett *46*; Ambrose Greenway, by courtesy of the Royal Navy Submarine Museum, Gosport *34*; Imperial War Museum, London *91* (below), 96–7; Lockheed Corporation, California, *128*; J. G. Moore Collection, London 13, 18 (both), 19, 27 (below right), 28–9, 58, 59 (above), 63, 74, *90* (above), *91* (above left & right), 100–1, 102–3, *116–17*, *128*, 129; Popperfoto, London 12, 15, 16 (both), 20–1, 25, 27 (above & below left), 30, 32–3, *34*, 37, 44, 45, 50, 52–3, 54–5, 59 (below), 60–1, 62, 66, 69, 70, 72, 73 (both), 78, 79, 80 (all), 81, *82–3*, 84, 85, *86*, 87, 89, *90* (below), 93, *95*, 106–7, 110–11, 114, 115, 118–19, *120–1*, 122–3 (all), *124–5*, 126, 127, 130–1, 132, 134, 136–7, 138–9; Radio Times Hulton Picture Library, London 10, 41, 49; Ann Ronan Picture Library *35* (both), *47* (bottom left); Royal Navy, London *113*; Eileen Tweedy *91* (below), *94*; US Navy Official Photograph, Washington, DC 13, 18, 19, 28–9, *116–17*; US Navy Collection in US National Archives, Washington, DC 100–1, 102–3.

All possible care has been taken in tracing the ownership of copyright material used in this book and making acknowledgement for its use. If any owner has not been acknowledged, the author and publishers apologize and will be glad of the opportunity to rectify the error.

Numerals in italics indicate colour photographs
Picture research by Popperfoto and J. G. Moore
Line drawings by Tony Garrett

Index